ROMAN
YORK

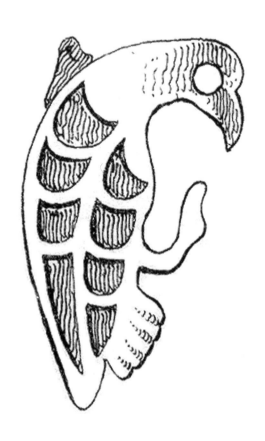

ROMAN
YORK

PATRICK OTTAWAY

The
History
Press

For Charmian with love
Coniugi Carissimae

Frontispiece: Drawing of a Roman brooch in the form
of a crow from C. Wellbeloved, *Eburacum* (1842)

First published 1993 by B.T. Batsford/English Heritage
This edition first published in 2004 by Tempus Publishing

Reprinted in 2011 by
The History Press
The Mill, Brimscombe Port
Stroud, Gloucestershire GL5 2QG
www.thehistorypress.co.uk

Reprinted 2013

British Library Cataloguing in Publication Data.
A catalogue record for this book is available from the British Library.

ISBN 978 0 7524 2916 8

Typesetting and origination by Tempus Publishing.
Printed and bound by TJ International Ltd, Padstow, Cornwall

CONTENTS

PREFACE TO THE SECOND EDITION

In the first edition of this book, published in 1993, I wrote that it was both a good time and a bad time to produce a book on Roman York. It was a good time because public and academic interest in the subject had probably never been greater, but a bad time, partly, at least, because research on most of the major archaeological excavations of what were then the previous twenty years or so was still in progress. On preparing this second edition some ten years later I felt the auguries were much more favourable because a good deal, although by no means all, of that research has been completed. For example, the great campaign of excavations under York Minster (1967-72), in which the legionary fortress headquarters and first cohort barracks were revealed, was published in 1995 by Derek Philips and Brenda Heywood. My own volume on the fortress defences (*Archaeology of York* 3/3) appeared in 1996 and we also have Jason Monaghan's wide-ranging survey of Roman pottery from York (*Archaeology of York* 16/8), published in 1997, which has made available a vast body of data relating to ceramic production and trade in *Eboracum*, and has also allowed the critical re-evaluation of archaeological dating for the period. In the first edition of this book I also referred to the problems inherent in having only a very small archaeologically excavated sample of the Roman settlement at York on which to make conclusions of a general nature. The sample remains small, but since 1993 there have been some important new excavations which have expanded knowledge of the subject considerably. For example, in 2002 two previously unrecorded Roman camps were discovered by aerial photography at Monk's Cross, about 5km (3 miles) north-east of York *(26)*; one was excavated and dated to the Hadrianic period, thereby prompting a renewed evaluation of York's role at this crucial period in the history of Roman Britain. There has also been work on the fortress defences in the York Archaeological Trust training excavation at St Leonard's Hospital which has revealed more of one of the interval towers (SW6) and a section through the adjacent rampart. Within the fortress, work at the Minster Library in 1997 revealed an important structural sequence and confirmed the location of a street *(79)*.

Readers familiar with the first edition will find the format and a good deal of the content of this new edition readily recognisable, but I am grateful to

Tempus Publishing for allowing me both to expand on certain topics to take account of recent research and to include others which had to be excluded for reasons of space the first time around. As a result, there has been an adjustment in terms of the relative length of the chapters. In particular, Chapters 3 and 4 have gained at the expense of Chapter 5 – Late Roman York – largely because construction of the defences in stone on the south-west and north-west sides of the fortress (p.72-5), and of the great public building, probably a bath house, at 1-9 Micklegate, south-west of the river Ouse (p.100) is now regarded, in both cases, as belonging to the early third century rather than to the late third or even early fourth century. Although these changes of dating may seem to be unsettling, because they require a recasting of a narrative previously seen as firmly founded, they do, at least, serve to re-emphasise the vibrant character of York at the time of the Severan emperors (197-235). They also show, as if one was in any doubt, that the story of Roman York is constantly unfolding. New discoveries and new analyses in the next ten years or so will probably render many of today's conclusions unsound or at least in need of modification and I, for one, look forward to seeing in what new directions we are taken.

P.J.C.O. New Year's Day 2004

ACKNOWLEDGEMENTS

As it was when I was completing the first edition in 1993, it is once again a pleasure to acknowledge the encouragement and support I have received in the preparation of this new one. I am, first of all, grateful to colleagues past and present at the York Archaeological Trust, in particular Peter Addyman and Richard Hall. In addition, thanks are due to Glenys Boyles, Martin Brann, Amanda Clarke, Hilary Cool, Rhona Finlayson, Kurt Hunter-Mann, Mark Johnson, Jason Monaghan, Niall Oakey and Nick Pearson. I owe a special debt of gratitude to Terry Finnemore, whose meticulous checking of detail was invaluable for my research on the Roman fortress plan. Terry has also drawn illustrations 23 and 34. In preparing the second edition I am grateful to my colleague Lesley Collett for her work on preparing new illustrations (1, 8, 15) and for re-drawing a number of others (13, 14, 38, 44, 47, 50, 53, 56, 64, 83). Mike Andrews assisted me with finding photographs in the Trust archive and making digital copies.

Outside the Trust I am most grateful to Professor Martin Millett, who read through the draft text of the first edition and made many useful comments and suggestions. My thanks are also due to Elizabeth Hartley, Keeper of Archaeology at the Yorkshire Museum and Melanie Baldwin, the Registrar, for making illustrations of items in the collections available. Louise Hampson and Peter Young generously assisted with images from the York Minster archive. Allan Hall, Andrew Jones, Harry Kenward and Terry O'Connor, past and present fellows of the Environmental Archaeology Unit at the University of York, kindly provided information on matters concerning their specialist interests.

COPYRIGHT OF ILLUSTRATIONS

York Minster: 6; colour plate: 15
Dr R.F.J. Jones: 10-11
English Heritage, Crown Copyright: 26, 28-9, 66-7, 69, 71-2
Field Archaeology Services, University of York: 79
Royal Archaeological Institute and York Archaeological Trust: 81
Illustration 43 appears courtesy of M.J. Jones, City Archaeologist for Lincoln
Illustration 5 was given to the author by the late L.P. Wenham
Author's copyright: 16-17, 30, 32-3, 42, 57, 73, 86; colour plates: 1-3, 6, 8,
    9, 13

CHAPTER 1

THE SEARCH FOR ROMAN YORK – 'A PLACE OF GREAT IMPORTANCE'

The City of York, known to the Romans as *Eboracum* (or *Eburacum*), owes its origins to the Ninth Legion which is thought to have arrived in the year AD 71 and to have built a great fortress on the north-east bank of the river Ouse. In about the year 120 the Ninth Legion was replaced by the Sixth, which remained, nominally at least, as the garrisoning force until the end of the Roman period in the early fifth century. During the second century York also became the site of a major urban settlement. One part lay on the north-east bank of the Ouse and the other on the south-west bank. By the early third century this settlement had become a provincial capital and acquired the status of a *colonia*, a largely honorific title by this time, but at least showing that York had received a measure of imperial favour denied to most other places in Britain. This dual character, with military and civilian sites of the highest rank side by side, makes *Eboracum* unique in Britain and crucial for the understanding of the Roman imperial achievement in this country.

The importance of Roman York is underlined by the documented visits of two emperors, both of whom died here. The first of these imperial casualties was Septimius Severus, who used York as a campaign base in the years 208-11, and the second was Constantius I who died in 306. Following Constantius's death, his son Constantine I ('the Great') was acclaimed as emperor by the army in York *(colour plates 2 and 11)*. These great events, which thrust York on to the world's stage, have given an added edge to local pride over the years, leading William Hargrove, a newspaper proprietor and journalist, for example, to open his *History of York*, published in 1818, as follows:

> In the earliest records of English History, *Ebor*, *Eboracum* or York, is represented as a place of great importance; and, in the zenith of meridian splendour, it was the residence of Imperial Power, and the legislative seat of the Roman Empire. Hence we may readily suppose, especially when the ancient historic accounts of this city are contrasted with those of London, that York far exceeded in dignity and consequence, if not in population and extent, the present capital of the British Empire, at that period.

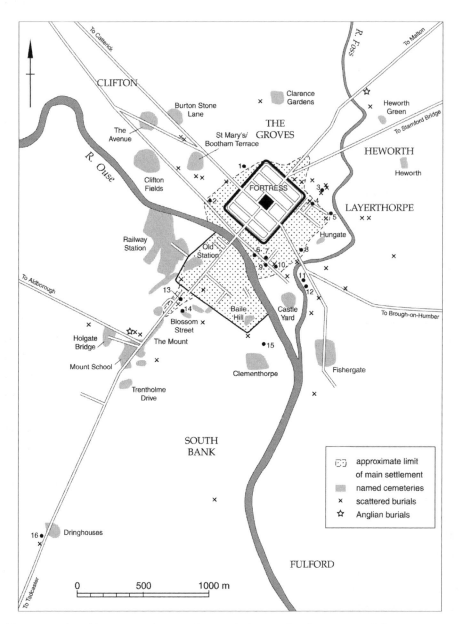

1 Map of Roman York and its environs showing the principal areas of settlement, recorded cemeteries (named) and scattered burials, and selected roads and streets (known and conjectured)

Key to sites outside the fortress and the principal civilian settlement (*colonia*) south-west of the Ouse:

1 31-7 Gillygate: timber building
2 St Mary's Abbey: street and buildings
3 County Hospital, Foss Bank: ditches and burials
4 21-33 Aldwark: burial, streets and building with mosaic
5 Borthwick Institute and Peasholme Green: kiln waste dumps
6 39-41 Coney Street: grain warehouse

and street
7 Spurriergate/High Ousegate: street and buildings including baths
8 Garden Place: structure and river inlet?
9 Former Barclay's Bank, Nessgate: buildings and dedications to Hercules and the imperial numen
10 16- 22 Coppergate: buildings and burials/St Mary Castlegate: mosaic

11 38 Piccadilly: Roman river bank
12 50 Piccadilly: Roman river bank
13 14-20 Blossom Street: road, street and buildings
14 35-41 Blossom Street: ditches and cemetery
15 Clementhorpe: house
16 The 'Starting Gate', Dringhouses: road and building

While such hyperbole is out of fashion amongst historians today, the Roman period still captures the imagination as powerfully as any other period of York's history; indeed the status the city acquired in the late first century has influenced almost every aspect of its subsequent development. After Britain had ceased to be part of the Roman Empire, York was to retain a pre-eminent role in the economic, military, political and religious affairs of the north of England in the succeeding Anglian, Anglo-Scandinavian and medieval periods. Although it has to be admitted that York's economic and political dominance had begun to decline by the end of Elizabeth I's reign, the Church and the Army have retained York as northern headquarters to the present day. In the mid-nineteenth century York returned to a position of regional economic importance as a railway centre and during the reign of Elizabeth II it has become a thriving city of over 100,000 inhabitants with a diverse economy based not only on engineering and the manufacture of chocolate, but also on new technologies with centres at York University and elsewhere. In addition, tourism focused on the museums and historic sites provides an ever-increasing contribution to the city's income.

It is, of course, in the nature of things that a place which has been occupied for almost two thousand years should see the buildings, streets and monuments of one generation demolished and built over by the next. As a result there is little of Roman York to be seen above ground today, but a flavour of former glories can still be enjoyed at three locations in the former fortress. At its very heart, displayed where they were unearthed in advance of work to support the Minster tower, can be seen the remains of the legionary *principia* or headquarters building. A column from the great hall, or basilica, has been re-erected outside the south door of the Minster *(colour plate 1)*. At the east corner of the fortress stands the fine walling of the defences, which probably dates to the late second century *(32)*. Finally, in the Museum Gardens is the Multangular Tower standing at the west corner of the fortress, which together with the adjacent stretches of the curtain wall, forms one of the most impressive witnesses to the military power of the Roman Empire to be found anywhere in western Europe *(80 and colour plates 3 and 6)*. In addition, the nearby Yorkshire Museum boasts a remarkable collection of Roman antiquities ranging from fine stone sculpture to grave finds such as pottery vessels and jewellery made of bone, jet and precious metals.

There are no other upstanding Roman remains in York, but the medieval city walls to the north-east and north-west of the Minster directly overlie the defences of the fortress while two of York's principal thoroughfares, Stonegate and Petergate, run close to the line of important Roman streets. South-west of the Ouse the medieval walls are also likely to overlie Roman defences and Micklegate Bar, in origin an eleventh-century gateway, probably stands close to the site of a Roman predecessor.

The earliest written reference to York is datable to about the year 100 and occurs as an address on one of the famous wooden writing tablets from Vindolanda, a fort near Hadrian's Wall. It occurs here in the form *Eburacum*, as it does in the Antonine Itinerary and Ravenna Cosmography, two road books of the Roman period which give place-names along the principal highways of the empire. The form *Eboracum* is, however, a little more common, occurring, for example, in the works of the second-century Greek geographer Ptolomy and on several inscriptions on stone from York. The second spelling is used in this book and is still current today, usually in its abbreviated form '*Ebor*', in, for example, the signature of the archbishop and the name of the principal race meeting on the Knavesmire featuring the great Ebor handicap over 1 mile 6 furlongs. The original meaning of *Eboracum* is uncertain, but it may derive from a British word meaning 'the place of the yew trees'.

The Vindolanda address is one of only about thirty or so written references to York in literary and epigraphic sources, many of which tell us little else of historic value. What is known of the history of Roman York is, therefore, based almost entirely on archaeological evidence. Since much of this evidence is buried and unseen, it is worth outlining some of its characteristics by way of an introduction to the discoveries themselves. The archaeology of York is made up, firstly, of abandoned structures in varying states of incompleteness and, secondly, of a vast number of superimposed layers of building debris, domestic and industrial refuse, ancient garden soil and the like, which are testimony to the intensity of human activity in the city over the centuries. Within the city centre there is typically about 3-5m (10-16ft) of archaeology below modern ground level. The depth of buried structures and deposits poses serious technical problems for archaeologists, requiring, for example, the use of expensive shoring to keep trench sides safe. The remains of the Roman period, usually buried more deeply than those of later times, are however relatively well-preserved from damage by modern intrusions, such as cellars and service trenches. Another factor favouring preservation of archaeological material arises from York's low-lying situation, which means that it has been greatly affected by a gradual rise in the water table since Roman times. In many areas of the city the ground has become waterlogged and this has ensured the remarkable and unusual survival of organic materials, from timber buildings to insect and plant remains.

Although the archaeology of York can be seen as an archive, it is of course unlike the papers in a book which can be consulted time and time again. Every time we read a page of the buried past in the course of excavation, either deliberately for research purposes or accidentally for construction and the like, we are destroying that past, and the thorough recording of any discoveries is therefore vital. It is fortunate that in York, as in Britain's other historic towns, there has been a long history of investigating the buried remains of the past. A continuous thread links the early antiquaries of the sixteenth and seventeenth centuries, who recovered individual objects of intrinsic artistic or historic interest, such as coins, jewellery and tombstones, to the archaeologists of today who adhere to a rigorous academic discipline demanding the highest standards in recording and publication.

ROMAN YORK — A HISTORY OF RESEARCH

The first scholar of national reputation to draw attention to Roman York was probably the Tudor geographer and historian William Camden. In his *Britannia* (first published 1587), a unique survey of the country's historical sites and monuments, Camden noted such items as a stone coffin (since lost) of Verecundius Diogenes, a *sevir augustalis* (priest of the cult of the deified emperor), apparently brought to light in 1579. Amongst other early discoveries was that of an altar dedicated to Jupiter found in 1638 in Bishophill Senior on the south-west bank of the Ouse and the tombstone of the standard-bearer Lucius Duccius Rufinus found in 1688 at Holy Trinity Church in Micklegate *(2)*.

In the eighteenth and nineteenth centuries many distinguished York residents interested themselves in the city's Roman remains. They included Martin Lister (1638?-1712), the eminent zoologist who was a polymath true to the spirit of his times. He contributed papers on such discoveries as the Bishophill altar to the Philosophical Transactions of the Royal Society. Lister was also the first person to recognise the Multangular Tower as a Roman structure and his work formed one of the sources for a great landmark in the study of York's history. Entitled *Eboracum*, but covering other periods as well as the Roman, this was published in 1736 by Francis Drake (1696-1771), a local surgeon. As a correspondent of the great antiquary William Stukeley, creator of much of the mythology surrounding the druids, Drake, like many other amateur scholars of his time, combined a curiosity about the past and a desire to record its remains with fanciful speculation and misplaced civic pride. This led him, for example, erroneously to assert that the emperor Constantine the Great had actually been born in York and that Helena his mother was British.

2 Tombstone of the Ninth Legion standard bearer Lucius Duccius Rufinus from Vienne in the Rhône valley, France (height 1.88m). Found at Holy Trinity Micklegate in 1688

3 Illustration from Wellbeloved's *Eburacum*, published 1842. The Mithraic relief *(left)* was found in Micklegate in 1747 and the dedication tablet from the temple of Serapis was found in Toft Green in 1770. The latter reads: 'to the holy god Serapis' – DEO SANCTO SERAPI – 'Claudius Hieronymianus, legate of the sixth legion victorious, built this temple from the ground' – A SOLO FECIT. (Relief: height 0.68m; tablet: width 0.91m)

In 1818 William Hargrove published the history of York quoted earlier, which reviewed previous discoveries and such new material as the Mithraic relief found in 1747 near St Martin-cum-Gregory Church and the inscription from a temple of Serapis found on Toft Green in 1770 *(3)*. The search for Roman York was continued by the Reverend Charles Wellbeloved (1769-1858), a Unitarian minister who was also one of the founders of the Yorkshire Philosophical Society in 1822 and the first honorary curator of antiquities in the Society's Museum, known today as the Yorkshire Museum. In 1842 Wellbeloved published his *Eburacum*, based both on previous discoveries and first-hand observation *(3 and 70)*. For example, he included the discovery of the fortress defences destroyed during the creation of St Leonard's Place and Exhibition Square in 1835. Wellbeloved also correctly surmised the limits of the legionary fortress – or 'city' as he called it – although they were not finally demonstrated by excavation until the 1950s. In addition, *Eburacum* contains extensive descriptions of discoveries in the 'suburbs' on the south-west bank of the Ouse, notably remains of a great baths complex of which more was revealed during the building of the first railway station (the 'Old Station') in 1839-40. This involved making a breach in the medieval and Roman defences and was perhaps the most devastating single episode of destruction ever suffered by York's archaeology.

A great deal was also destroyed during the latter half of the nineteenth and early twentieth centuries, when York grew rapidly as a result of its new-found role as a railway centre. One of the more important discoveries was part of a great commemorative inscription of the reign of the emperor Trajan, found in

4 The commemorative inscription found in King's Square. It is the latest dated reference to the Ninth Legion and can be ascribed to the year December 107-December 108. The dedication to Trajan gives his titles as 'Emperor Caesar, son of the divine Nerva, Nerva Traianus, Augustus, Germanicus, Dacicus (commemorating his victories in Dacia, now Romania), chief priest' – IM]P(ERATOR) CAESAR DIVI [N]ERVAE FIL(IVS) N[ERVA TRAI]ANVS AUG(VSTVS) GER[M(ANICVS) DACICVS [PO]NTIFEX MAXIMV[S. Dating is derived from the reference to Trajan being in his twelfth year of tribunician power, fifth year as imperator and fifth year as consul – TRIBVNICIAE [PO] TESTATIS XII IMP(ERATOR) V [CO(N) S(VL) V. Reference to the legion is in the last line where the work commemorated, possibly a gate, is described as – PER LEG(IONEM) VIIII HI[SP(ANAM) FECIT. (Height: 1.14m)

King's Square in 1854 during work on York's first main sewers *(4)*. In the 1870s another redoubtable clergyman-antiquary, the Reverend James Raine, curator of antiquities at the Yorkshire Museum 1873-96, observed the massive earthmoving operations undertaken for the present railway station which disturbed one of the principal cemeteries of the Roman *colonia*. At much the same time the creation of the fashionable suburb on The Mount outside Micklegate Bar led to the discovery of more of the fine funerary monuments which had originally lined the main Roman road to York from the south-west *(69, 72, colour plate 10)*.

The first systematic archaeological excavations in Roman York were conducted in the 1920s under the direction of Stuart Miller, a lecturer at Glasgow University, on behalf of the York Excavation Committee. This was a body newly formed along the lines of a number of others which emerged in historic towns around Britain at this time. Between 1925 and 1928 Miller addressed himself primarily to the fortress defences and it was while digging at the east corner that he revealed, preserved beneath the medieval rampart, the stretch of fortress wall standing some 5m (16ft) high which can still be seen today *(32)*. Other early excavations revealed part of the fortress baths in St Sampson's Square in 1930-1, and, in advance of the construction of an Air Raid Control Centre in 1939, more of the baths previously encountered when the first railway station was built.

During the 1950s and 1960s, a time in which the pace of redevelopment in the city increased considerably, much of the burden of investigating York's archaeology was borne by volunteers, although their resources were usually very restricted. One of the most active excavators of the period was Peter Wenham,

5 Excavations in progress on a Roman house at St Mary Bishophill Junior *c.*1964 under the direction of L.P. Wenham (kneeling centre with tape)

6 Roman column from the basilica of the legionary fortress headquarters found during the excavations under York Minster. This has now been re-erected outside the south door of the Minster *(colour plate 1)*

head of history at St John's College *(5)*. His work included investigation of the site of the Davygate shopping arcade from 1955 to 1958 (Site 21 on *13*) where he recorded the fortress defences and four legionary barrack blocks (which he designated S, P, Q and R!). Wenham's most extensive excavation, however, took place at Trentholme Drive in 1951-2 and 1957-9, about 1.5km (0.9 mile) south-west of Micklegate Bar where he found a substantial Roman cemetery, the first in York to be examined archaeologically rather than unearthed in building work.

Archaeological work in the 1950s was also undertaken by the staff of the Royal Commission on Historical Monuments for England (hereafter RCHME) as a part of their great inventory of the city. The first volume, *Eburacum*, which appeared in 1962, is a thorough catalogue and evaluation of all discoveries of the Roman period made up to that date. It remains a vital source for research into Roman York, although its conclusions now require modification in many respects. The RCHME was also involved in excavations at the Minster in the heart of the legionary fortress where the danger of collapse of the central tower rendered major ground works necessary. Archaeological work began in 1967 and was completed in 1972 by Derek Philips, who became the York Minster archaeologist. Initially, the aim of the Minster excavations was to locate the Anglo-Saxon Minster referred to by the Venerable Bede as the site of King Edwin of Northumbria's baptism in 627. As time went on, however, and Edwin's church did not appear, other research topics including the Roman fortress headquarters were given attention, and in due course it was decided that the Roman walls should be put on public display. Although work could only proceed in small areas during restoration and conditions were difficult, if not dangerous, the complete sequence of development of the headquarters basilica and adjacent barracks, from the first to the fifth century and beyond, was discovered *(6)*.

While work was beginning at the Minster, RCHME had moved on to the next volume of its York inventory, which was concerned with the city's defences. In connection with this work Jeffrey Radley set about re-excavating a stone tower built into the Roman fortress wall near the Multangular Tower. This was first discovered in 1842 when the Recorder of York had by chance driven a tunnel through it to get access to his stables in King's Manor. Radley suggested that the tower was post-Roman and it is now officially known as the 'Anglian Tower', although for reasons which will be discussed below, the tower is more likely to be late Roman *(80)*. Subsequent to the excavation York City Council decided to put the tower on permanent display and, in addition, as part of the celebrations which took place in 1971 to commemorate 1900 years of York since its foundation by the Romans, exposed an adjacent stretch of the fortress wall by removing the overlying medieval rampart.

In spite of the discoveries outlined above, the overall picture of archaeological work in York in the late 1960s and early 1970s was one of an inadequate response to the threat posed by modern development. Projects were dealt with on an individual basis and there was no body with overall strategic or academic responsibility. The 'rescue archaeology' crisis in York acquired a new urgency in 1968 with the publication of Lord Esher's report entitled *York: A Study in Conservation*, which led to plans for an inner ring-road. While it was the intention to avoid above-ground historic buildings the road threatened large areas of rich below-ground archaeology immediately outside the city walls including Roman cemeteries and suburbs. At this point the Council for British Archaeology and the Yorkshire Philosophical Society, the latter imbued no doubt with the spirit of its founder member, Reverend Wellbeloved, sponsored the formation of the York Archaeological Trust (YAT). This was set up in April 1972 with funds from the Department of the Environment and assistance and premises from York University.

The Trust was an organisation comparable to a number of others set up at about the same time to tackle archaeology in important historic towns. Its work has involved, first of all, excavation in advance of new building and other construction work, and also the monitoring of all other disturbances of the ground caused, for example, by trenches for gas, sewage and other services. Fieldwork has, however, been guided by specific research objectives within what found-ing Trust Director, Peter Addyman, described as a 'broadly based examination of the whole process of urbanisation over the past two millennia'. The study of Roman York has, of course, had a major part to play in this and since 1972 a wide range of projects has added enormously to our understanding of the sub-ject. A brief summary of some of the more significant discoveries by the Trust and by other organisations who have worked in York recently may serve to prepare the reader for more detailed discussion in the following chapters.

RECENT EXCAVATIONS AND RESEARCH

As far as the Roman fortress is concerned, work has, as before 1972, been mostly small scale, but has included further examination of the defences and adjacent areas, in the first instance, near the east corner in the Aldwark/Bedern area in advance of the urban renewal proposed by Esher. In the central part of the fortress, rescue work in Church Street in 1972 revealed the great sewer which served the bath house (Site 15 on *13*; *18*), and an excavation at 9 Blake Street (Site 17 on *13*) in 1975 produced a sequence of buildings and a street *(21 and 41)*. In 1997 an excavation by York University archaeologists examined build-ings and a street near the north corner in advance of construction of the Minster Library extension (Site 4 on *13*; *79*). Important work also took place on the south-western fortress defences in 1996 at Davygate and at St Leonard's Hospital adjacent to Interval Tower SW6 in 2001-3, the latter in a training excavation which grew out of a three-day project (September 1–3, 1999) by the well-known television programme *Time Team*. Although large areas of the fortress will remain inaccessible for archaeological examination below the historic build-ings of the city centre, the small excavation sites and watching briefs which have been possible in the last 30 years have, as will be shown in the next two chapters, allowed much of the plan of the late first-century fortress to be determined along with aspects of the changes in layout which took place in the second century.

Study of the Roman civilian settlements has been concentrated on the opposite bank of the Ouse to the fortress and has formed one of the Archaeological Trust's most coherent research projects within the rescue framework. This began in 1973 with the examination of the remains of a large town house sited on an artificial terrace in the south-eastern part of the settlement at 37 Bishophill Senior (Site 23 on *44*). On the adjacent 58-9 Skeldergate site (Site 25 on *44*) a remarkably well-preserved timber-lined well was discovered *(68)*. Its conservation had an important part to play in the development of techniques for the treatment of waterlogged wood from archaeological sites, in which the Trust's conservation laboratory has become an internationally recognised centre of excellence. In addition, the contents of the well were highly organic and included abundant plant remains, animal bones and even micro-organisms from the human gut. This material provided one of the first indications of the potential in York for understanding the ecology of Roman settlement and the subject has been one of the principal research themes of the Environmental Archaeology Unit established by the Trust and the Inspectorate of Ancient Monuments at York University.

In 1981 the archaeological potential of Roman York south-west of the Ouse was further revealed by a small trench at 5 Rougier Street close to the main approach road to York from the south-west *(50-1)*. The site produced a 3m (10ft) depth of Roman deposits and demonstrated the existence of a well-preserved buried Roman townscape in this hitherto unexplored part of the city. In 1983-4 more extensive trenches were dug in the same area in advance of an extension to the offices of General Accident Assurance (now part of Aviva) on the corner of Rougier Street and Tanner Row *(53-5)*. This was one of the first excavations in York to receive substantial funding from the site developers themselves. Previously, funding for the Trust's excavation work had been largely provided by central and local government, but since the early 1980s it has become the norm at York, in line with practice elsewhere in the country, for developers to bear the principal cost burden of rescue archaeology.

The General Accident, Tanner Row site produced remarkable remains of late second-century timber buildings with their associated artefact-rich refuse heaps. The trenches here were narrow, however, and complete building plans could not be determined. Fortunately a much larger area became available in May 1988 at the nearby Wellington Row site where excavations directed by the author continued for much of the next two years *(45-8)*. The first major discovery here was the main Roman road from the south-west at a crucial point where it approached the crossing over the Ouse. Alongside the road the remains of a substantial stone building were uncovered. It had had a long and chequered history from the mid-second to the late fourth century, presenting in many ways a microcosm of the history of the settlement itself. At much the same time, part of a massive public building, probably a second bath house, emerged at 1-9 Micklegate (Queen's Hotel) in another previously unexplored area of the Roman town near Ouse Bridge *(63-4)*. One stretch of wall here survived standing to a height of 4m (13ft), making it one of York's most impressive archaeological finds and providing a foretaste of what may be found in any future investigations in the vicinity.

As a result of problems in securing access and funding for the excavations at the 1-9 Micklegate site, a changed relationship between archaeology and new development in the city emerged, guided by advice on archaeology's place in the planning process from central government. This, in turn, has had a profound effect on the direction the study of Roman York (and of York in other periods) has taken. Under provisions established by the city authorities for the preservation of archaeological remains, developers are required to make an archaeological evaluation of the sites on which they propose to build. This has meant the excavation of large numbers of small trenches in and around the city to test the depth and nature of archaeological remains. On the basis of the information derived from evaluation, developers are expected to put in place a strategy to minimise damage to the remains if at all possible, although destruction of 5% is considered acceptable. In the city centre this has usually meant building on thin piles driven through the archaeology. As a result, since the beginning of the 1990s there have been no large-scale excavation projects in the city centre of the sort undertaken in advance of development in the 1970s and 1980s at sites like Wellington Row. It is nonetheless the case that, because development has proceeded strongly in all parts of York, central and suburban, numerous windows into hitherto unexplored parts of the Roman settlement have been, at least, briefly opened. Of particular interest and value in the last ten years have been the opportunities to examine areas immediately outside the fortress and principal civilian settlements. In addition, parts of the Roman cemeteries have been excavated for the first time since the 1950s. For example, another component of the *Time Team* project in 1999 was work in the Roman cemetery adjacent to the railway station in the grounds of what was then the Royal York Hotel, as part of an important excavation by On Site Archaeology.

Since 1995 the City of York has been governed as a Unitary Authority which includes 31 parishes around it and the advantage of this has been a co-ordinated approach to the curation and management of its archaeological resources as far as the planning process is concerned. In respect of archaeological research, however, a disadvantage of the current arrangements is that there is no effective provision for a co-ordinated approach since developers usually invite competitive tenders for fieldwork projects. This has allowed a proliferation of archaeological organisations working in the York area, each of which usually controls the archive (finds and records) from its own discoveries and works to its own priorities for the dissemination of results. Although these archives may one day be managed by a single institution, a challenge for the present generation of archaeologists is to find a way of bringing together the results of excavations by the various organisations operating locally in such a way as to allow research into York's past to proceed effectively. Since 1995, for example, no fewer than four separate bodies have excavated, in total, well over a hundred Roman burials in York. How a research programme which would study and publish the material recovered, including the artefacts and human remains, is to be co-ordinated and funded remains far from clear. Another challenge which will not be easily met is to complete the analysis and publication of a number of important sites excavated in the 1980s at, for example, 1-9 Micklegate and Wellington Row. Should there be a third edition to this book in another ten years or so, it is to be hoped that the response to these challenges will be satisfactorily documented.

CHAPTER 2

THE FIRST FORTRESS

SETTING THE SCENE

When Quintus Petilius Cerialis, commander of the Ninth Legion, pitched his tent at what was to become *Eboracum* in about the year AD 71, he must have felt remote from the civilised world. Not only was he on an island beyond the great and terrible ocean, but he was also a long way from the fledgling Roman province, now some 25 years old, in the south of Britain where a semblance of a Roman way of life was beginning to emerge. When Vespasian became emperor in the year AD 69 the Roman province of *Britannia* had reached a line running roughly from the river Humber in the east to the river Mersey in the west, although north Wales was not finally pacified for another ten years.

Northern England as far as the Scottish Lowlands was largely occupied by a people known to the Romans as the Brigantes. Rather than belonging to a unified nation in any sense, however, they were probably little more than a loose confederation linked by dynastic ties. The Brigantian population was scattered in isolated farmsteads and small villages. There were apparently, with one exception, no communal centres (or *oppida*) comparable to those such as *Verulamium* (at St Albans) or *Camulodunum* (at Colchester) which the Romans had encountered in southern England. The exception is at Stanwick, near Richmond, North Yorkshire, where an area of some 300ha (741 acres) was enclosed by a great bank and ditch. Excavations at Stanwick by Sir Mortimer Wheeler in the 1950s and by Durham University more recently have produced Roman pottery, tile and other artefacts, such as glass, which date from the mid-first century. The implication of these discoveries is that Stanwick was a seat of a Brigantian aristocracy which had come under the influence of Roman civilisation and eagerly sought its material benefits. (The location of Stanwick is shown along with other sites in the York region mentioned in the text on map 8.)

Our knowledge of the occasion, or pretext, for the Roman attack on Brigantia comes from the works of the author Tacitus who, writing in the late first century, referred to a conflict between two parties in the Brigantian royal house which threatened the stability of the province to the south. On one side was Queen Cartimandua, who favoured good relations with the Romans, and on the other was her estranged husband Venutius, who led an anti-Roman party. Trouble had been brewing since as early as the year 51, when Cartimandua had handed over to the Romans the fugitive British rebel leader Caratacus after his defeat in Wales. Under the governor Didius Gallus (52-7) fortifications were apparently built in the frontier zone between what was then the Roman province and Brigantia. They included a fort at Templeborough, near Rotherham, and a fortress for part of a legion (a 'vexil-lation') at Rossington Bridge, 7km (4 miles) south of Doncaster. Subsequently, we hear that matters were made worse when the queen took Venutius's armour bearer, Vellocatus, as a lover. The outbreak of civil strife led to Roman intervention and 'at the cost of desperate fighting', as Tacitus puts it, Cartimandua was rescued from Venutius's forces.

One reason for the choice of York as a fortress site must have been that it was ideally placed to allow the army to strike at centres of native resistance in the valleys of the Pennines and North York Moors. The site may also have had the advantage of lying on the boundary between the Brigantes and another native people, the Parisi, who occupied an area roughly equivalent to the old East Riding of Yorkshire. In other words, York was perhaps in a neutral zone from where both peoples could be supervised, but not unduly provoked.

Another advantage of the York site was that it allowed for easy communications by land and water. As far as land communications are concerned, York lies on a glacial moraine – a ridge of rocky debris left by retreating glaciers after the last Ice Age. The moraine had been used since the Late Neolithic (i.e. from about 3000 BC) as a route across the low-lying and, in places, marshy Vale of York between the Wolds in the east and the Pennines in the west. York also lies at junction of this land route with the river Ouse at a point where it could be easily crossed. Finally, the Ouse provided a navigable route, via the Humber estuary, for ships bringing men and supplies from the east coast and North Sea some 60km (38 miles) distant.

When one considers the immediate environs of York it becomes apparent that the Roman military surveyors had an unerring talent for assessing a site's potential. The fortress was not only close to the junction of the rivers Ouse and Foss, which offered a natural defence on two sides, but it also stood on a slightly raised plateau, a prominent position in the local landscape which would have been more obvious in Roman times, when river levels were lower than they are today. It is difficult to determine those levels exactly and it should be recalled that they were subject to strong tidal influence which, since the mid-eighteenth century, has been restricted by Naburn lock downstream from York. Recent small-scale excavations on the south-west bank of the Ouse (e.g. at Site 26 on *44*) and the east bank of the Foss (Sites 11 and 12 on *1*) suggest, however, that in the late first century river levels may have been as much as 3m (10ft) below the present summer average of about 5m

7 Ceramic tile with the stamp of the Ninth Legion Hispana

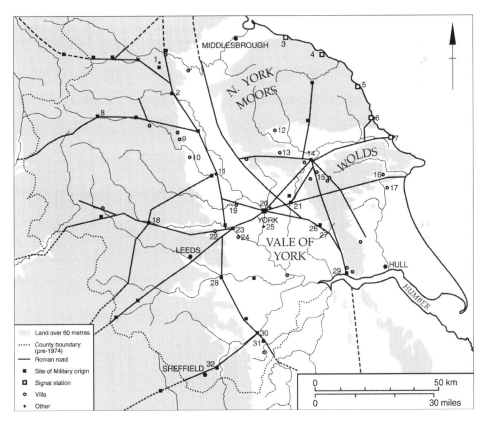

8 Map of Roman Yorkshire showing principal military sites, towns, villas and other settlements (modern cities shown for location purposes). Those referred to in text are as follows:

1 Stanwick	8 Bainbridge	14 Malton	21 Stamford Bridge	27 Shiptonthorpe	32 Templeborough
2 Catterick	9 Well	15 Langton	22 Dalton Parlours	28 Castleford	
3 Huntcliff	10 Castle Dykes,	16 Rudston	23 Tadcaster	29 Brough-on-	
4 Goldsborough	North Stainley	17 Harpham	24 Kirkby Wharfe	Humber	
5 Ravenscar	11 Aldborough	18 Ilkley	25 Lingcroft Farm,	30 Doncaster	
6 Scarborough	12 Beadlam	19 Wilstrop	Naburn	31 Rossington	
7 Filey	13 Hovingham	20 Appletree Farm	26 Hayton	Bridge	

(16ft) OD (above Ordnance Datum). The course of the rivers in Roman times is not altogether certain, but the Ouse has probably not changed a great deal over the centuries. The Foss was substantially altered by the creation of the King's Fish Pool in the late eleventh century after the Norman Conquest, and by canalisation in more recent times. In addition, excavations have shown that in Roman times the banks of the Foss, as it passed through York, sloped down much more steeply to water level than is apparent today.

On the south-west bank of the Ouse, where the principal Roman civilian settlement was to emerge, ground level in the valley bottom was several metres lower than in the fortress. A cross-section of the Ouse valley at York (*9*) shows that the natural ground surface only rises slightly for a distance of up to about 150m (164 yards) from the river bank, but then rises quite sharply to the south-west for about 300m (330 yards) before levelling off or dipping away slightly towards the line of the present city walls which are thought to be on the line of Roman defences (see p.90).

It appears that there was no permanent native settlement in what is now the city's historic core when the Romans arrived and the legion probably encountered a pleasant meadowland environment not unlike that on the upper reaches of the Ouse today. Research on well-preserved organic material,

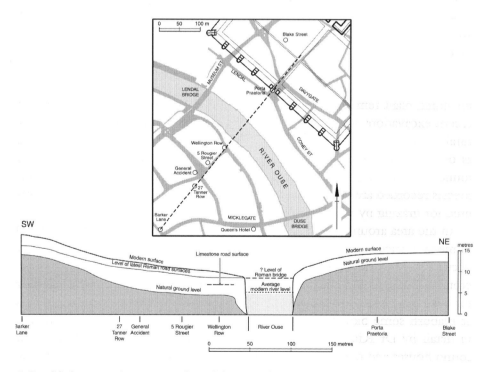

9 Simplified cross-section across York (with location plan) from Barker Lane (south-west) to Blake Street (north-east) along the line of the main Roman road from the south-west and *via praetoria* showing approximate ground and river levels in the Roman period

10 Aerial view of the late Iron Age/Roman settlement at Lingcroft Farm, Naburn showing the enclosure in Site A (see *11*)

including plant remains and snail shells, from the earliest deposits examined in recent excavations suggests a mixture of woodland scrub and cleared agricultural land. Deposits from sites close to the south-west bank of the Ouse have, as one would expect, produced the remains of organisms which are usually found on river banks, and in marshes and ponds. Many of the wetland plant species recorded are rather low-growing which may indicate that the land was used for grazing by native farmers.

In the area around York excavation and aerial photography have identified numerous traces of pre-Roman settlements, many of which were probably occupied at the time the Roman army arrived. They would have provided the crops and beasts needed to feed 5,000 or more hungry soldiers, and the labour for road building and other menial tasks. One of these so-called 'native' sites at Naburn some 5km (3 miles) south of the city centre has been examined in detail by Dr Rick Jones of Bradford University *(10-11)*. The remains of round houses and the rectangular enclosures defined by ditches in which they stood have been excavated (sites A, B and D). These features are dated to the late pre-Roman Iron Age. The houses do not seem to have survived into the Roman period itself, but the surrounding field system remained in use. Details

27

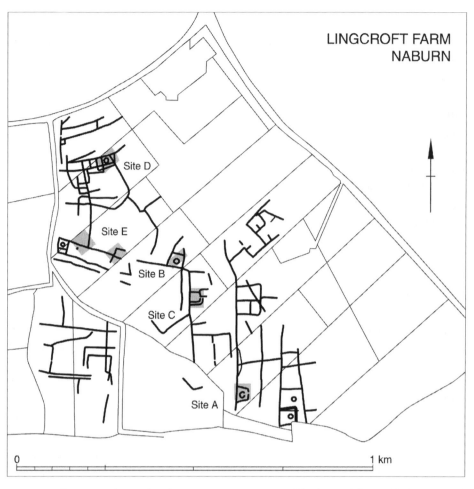

LINGCROFT FARM
NABURN

Site D

Site E

Site B

Site C

Site A

0   1 km

11 Lingcroft Farm, Naburn: plan showing excavation sites and landscape features identified from aerial photographs

12 Rawcliffe Moor: late Iron Age site with the remains of round houses and enclosure ditches. The grid of narrow, straight trenches is modern as is the trench running from upper left to lower centre

of agricultural practices at Naburn are scarce as animal bone and other organic materials did not survive well in the acid ground, but a charred grain deposit provided evidence for the cultivation of barley and wheat.

The advantages of Naburn for settlement derived from its location on an island of sandy subsoil in the alluvial clay of the Vale of York. This clay has, until recently, been thought unsuitable for arable agriculture and therefore settlement in pre-Roman times. However it is now clear that this was not the case; a site on clay examined at Rawcliffe Moor in 1996, about 4.5 km (2.8 miles) north of the centre of York, yielded the remains of round houses and enclosure ditches dated to the late pre-Roman Iron Age *(12)*. Whether this site was occupied at the time the Romans arrived is uncertain, although reorganisation of the landscape by the Romans (see below, p.53) might be one reason for its abandonment.

THE FORTRESS AND ITS MEN

In the late first century the Roman army in Britain consisted of two sorts of troops: legionaries and auxiliaries. The invasion in AD 43 brought four legions to this country, but after about the year 87 there were three which formed a permanent garrison. Each legion was made up of some 5,000 infantrymen and a small number of cavalry. The auxiliary regiments, some of whom were infantry and some cavalry, were raised from subject peoples throughout the empire. They were made up into units about 500 or 1,000 strong. The legionaries were based in fortresses whilst the auxiliaries were largely based in forts, smaller establishments of which there are many examples in the York region and in Britain as a whole.

The principal function of a Roman fortress was to provide accommodation for the men and equipment of a legion. Although it had defences to prevent sudden attacks by hostile forces, a fortress was not like a medieval castle, primarily designed for defence, but was a base from which the army would go out to fight in the field where its superior discipline and weaponry could be brought to bear on the enemy. By the late first century AD fortresses had become fairly standardised in plan resembling a playing card, usually some 20ha (50 acres) in extent with a grid of streets and a suite of buildings which varied little in function and location from place to place. As far as Britain is concerned, York appears to be very similar in size and plan to the fortress at Caerleon in Gwent, south Wales, founded only a few years later in 74-8. Another good model against which to compare the evidence for the early fortress at York is Inchtuthil, one of the most extensively excavated fortresses, built in the year 83 on the banks of the river Tay near Perth in Scotland.

The organisation of a late first-century Roman legion should now be briefly summarised as it explains, in large part, the details of the fortress layout. The basic unit was the *contubernium* of eight men who shared a tent when on campaign and a pair of rooms in a fortress barrack. Ten *contubernia* made a century of 80 men who occupied a barrack block and were commanded by a centurion. Six centuries made up a cohort of 480 men and ten cohorts a legion. In the late first century the first cohort was of double strength (960 men) and it probably included the *immunes*, who were excused from fighting but had specialist tasks as, for example, clerks, surveyors, engineers and smiths.

All legionaries were Roman citizens with access to the privileges that status conferred. In the first century AD the vast majority of the population of the empire was made up of non-citizens and slaves who, it has been said, were subject to the law while citizens were protected by it. This meant, for example, that citizens had more secure rights to own and inherit property than non-citizens and in the event of wrongdoing could usually avoid the more humiliating punishments such as working in the mines or confronting wild beasts in the amphitheatre. The citizen body was, however, by no means homogeneous; some of its members were a good deal more privileged than others. Membership of the highest ranks, the senators and the knights, or equestrians, was based on a property and wealth qualification, although there was also a strong hereditary element.

The command structure of a legion was closely integrated with the career paths of men in the upper echelons of the imperial social hierarchy, paths which would take them into both military and governmental positions. The post of legionary commander, the legate (*legatus*), was reserved for a man of senatorial rank. He was usually in his thirties and would have been destined for the highest offices in the empire. The second in command, known as the *tribunus laticlavius*, would also have been of senatorial rank, but in his early twenties. The other five senior officers, *tribuni angusticlavii*, were from the equestrian order. The equestrian tribunes again had a wide range of careers in military or administrative posts open to them. These senior officers usually served for no more than three years in a post before moving on. The highest ranking officer in a more permanent position was the camp prefect (*praefectus castrorum*), who took charge of the organisation of the fortress, and of training and equipment. The camp prefect was supported by the centurions, who were responsible for their men on a day-to-day basis.

By the late first century soldiers usually signed on for 25 years of service. Although this might seem unduly long, a career as a legionary was much sought after as it was seen as a route to social advancement. Legionaries not only had a steady income, but on retirement were given a handsome golden handshake which might include land attached to one of the *coloniae* (principal towns in the empire – see p.83). Wealth in the form of land was the key to entering the governing classes. Another privilege given to legionaries below the rank of centurion on retirement was that they were free to contract officially recognised marriages. This does not mean that they led celibate lives while in service, however, and unofficial arrangements were made for lady-friends and children to live in civilian settlements adjacent to the fortresses. Centurions and senior officers were allowed to marry while serving and could live with their families in the fortresses themselves.

Soldiers were amongst those members of Roman society who had the funds and the inclination to make dedications to the gods or to the memory of their deceased colleagues by erecting inscribed stone monuments. We can therefore learn something of individual soldiers in York from altars and tombstones (see also p.58-61). Of the two tombstones which refer to men of the Ninth Legion, one is incomplete and so the soldier's name is unknown, but we do know that he came from Novaria in northern Italy and that his freedmen heirs set up the stone for a 'well-deserving patron'. These freedmen were probably the man's slaves given their liberty, or manumission, under the terms of his will and so we have an indication here of the personal wealth that some legionaries could command. The second Ninth Legion tombstone is one of the finest funerary monuments from York. It was erected for the standard-bearer (*signifer*) Lucius Duccius Rufinus *(2)*. He is shown holding a standard in his right hand and a case of writing tablets in his left which may represent his will. He wears a form of cloak known as a *paenula* over his body armour and around his neck is a torque, a necklet favoured by Gallic and British people of both sexes. The inscription tells us that Rufinus was a Gaul from Vienna (*Vienne*) in the Rhône valley and this serves to make the point that the men who came to York with the legion had diverse geographical origins. Whereas Julius Caesar's troops in the mid-first century BC came largely from Italy, Rufinus is typical of the soldiers drawn from Roman citizens in the Gallic and other provinces who were entering the army in large numbers by the late first century AD.

Another Ninth Legion inscription from York is to be found on an altar. It had been set up by the clerk (*cornicularius*) Celerinius Vitalis to Silvanus, a god of the woods and wild places. This seems an eminently appropriate dedication for a member of a legion that was campaigning in the wild and mysterious north, and whose favourite pastime was probably hunting the deer, wild boar and other game which abounded in local forests.

THE FOUNDATION OF THE FORTRESS

(The location of sites in the fortress is shown on *13*.)

The date of AD 71 usually given for the foundation of the legionary fortress at York is derived from analysis of the campaigns of the governors of Britain described by the author Tacitus in the biography of his father-in-law, Gnaeus Agricola (governor 78-84) rather than from archaeological evidence. However, whilst there is no archaeological reason at present to challenge this date, there

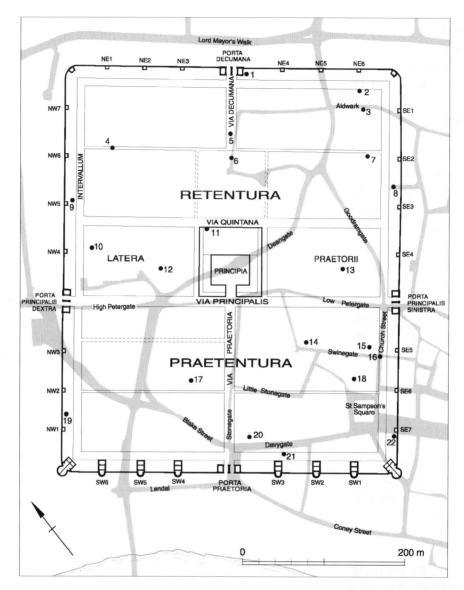

13 Plan of the Roman fortress at York showing its principal zones and the location of archaeological sites, other than those on the defences, referred to in the text. (The designation of the interval towers follows that of the Royal Commission on Historical Monuments for England)

1 Gray's Court: intervallum building
2 1-5 Aldwark: barracks
3 Bedern (Trench 1): barracks
4 Minster Library: street and barracks
5 Treasurer's House: via decumana
6 Chapter House Street: via decumana or entrance to praetorium
7 Bedern (Trench 5): buildings
8 Bedern (Trench 3-4): buildings and defences
9 Dean's Park: Interval Tower NW5 and intervallum building

10 Purey Cust Nursing Home: first cohort barracks
11 Minster Excavations: headquarters building
12 Minster Excavations: first cohort barracks
13 Hornpot Lane/Low Petergate: buildings
14 Swinegate: legionary baths
15 Church Street: legionary baths and sewer
16 Church Street: intervallum, street and wall

17 9 Blake Street: accommodation block, street and barracks
18 Roman Bath public house, St Sampson's Square: legionary baths caldarium
19 The 'Anglian Tower'
20 Border's bookshop, Davygate: barracks
21 Davygate: barracks and defences
22 16 Parliament Street and Parliament Street sewer trench

is some indication of military activity at York before the fortress was built. This has come primarily from excavations at 9 Blake Street where, below fortress buildings, there was a fairly substantial ditch (1.2m wide and 0.5m deep) dug into the natural clay subsoil on an east–west alignment, that is at 45° to the alignment of the fortress buildings above it. In the earliest infilling layer of this ditch a coin of the emperor Nero, dated to the year 66, was found along with pottery which could also belong to Nero's reign (54-68). This ditch, of unknown function, was cut by two pits of much the same date as the ditch. These features do not tell us much, but it is just possible they belonged to a base established at York by Vettius Bolanus, the governor before Petilius Cerialis, in the year 69 when the Romans had to rescue Cartimandua from Venutius.

While the status of any pre-fortress military establishment is as yet unknown, it can only have been short-lived and we may now turn to the layout of the fortress itself. The corners of the site were at the cardinal points (north, south, east and west) and so the prevailing alignments of the streets and buildings were north-east/south-west and north-west/south-east. These align-ments were subsequently to determine much of the layout of Roman York and, moreover, that of the city of York as we know it today.

The Roman army preferred sites for its fortifications which were as level as possible, and it has become clear from excavations that ground level within the fortress at York did not vary a great deal. It was at its highest in the centre and western quadrant, sloped down slightly to the east corner, and it was only towards the south corner that any marked slope occurred. At the site of the headquarters (at York Minster) natural ground level occurs at about 13.5m (44ft) OD, near the north corner it is 12.45m OD, at Interval Tower SW5, near the west corner, the natural level is about 14m (46ft) OD, near the east corner the level is about 12m (39ft) OD while in the area of the south corner it drops to about 11m (36ft) OD.

Once the site had been chosen, the fortress was carefully laid out and the legionary surveyors (*agrimensores*) probably had a manual giving them details of how this was to be done. There are two military surveying manuals which have survived from the Roman period: *De munationibus castrorum* by Hyginus, a writer of the mid-second century who describes how a camp was laid out at that time, and *Epitoma rei militaris* by Vegetius, a fourth-century author, who makes legion-ary camps his principal subject. These sources are of limited value, however, for understanding York's fortress in any detail; this must rely largely on archaeology. Having said this, restricted opportunities for excavation in a modern city mean that York's original late first century plan is not as well-known as, for example, that of Inchtuthil, noted above, where there is no later settlement. Nonetheless, by the late first-century British fortresses had become so standardised in plan that once the line of the defences and principal streets and the location of some of the more important buildings have been discovered, the rest of the plan of a site like York can be determined with some degree of confidence.

The Roman surveyor's principal instrument was the *groma*, which consisted of an iron cross with four arms at 90° to one another, each of which had a plumb line suspended from the end. Another line hung from the centre of the cross so that it could be set up over a fixed point in the ground. The cross was attached by a bracket to a staff which was positioned off-centre to enable the surveyor to sight through opposing plumb lines and, with the aid of ranging poles, survey straight lines and right angles. For the purposes of measuring, the surveyors had rules for shorter distances and, presumably, rods and chains for longer.

The main problem with using a *groma* was keeping the plumb lines still in windy conditions, but it appears that the Romans were able to survey with a reasonable degree of accuracy. Discrepancies still do appear in fortress plans, usually fairly minor, between the actual measurements on the ground and what we believe was the original blueprint. These may be due, on the one hand, to the inadequacies of the Roman surveying equipment or to adjustments to localised topographical problems. On the other hand archaeologists may themselves introduce inaccuracies where none actually existed; their survey work, especially on confined and enclosed sites in urban areas, is far from error free. None of these factors, however, obscures the evidence for a regularity in the plans of many Roman military sites, including the fortress at York *(14)* which is based on units of the Roman foot or *pes Monetalis* (1pM = about 0.296m or 0.97 imperial feet), so-called after the standard which was to be found in the temple of Juno Moneta in Rome.

One of the first tasks of the legionary surveyors was to decide the orientation of the headquarters building, or *principia*, which in turn determined the orientation of the fortress itself. At York the fortress faces south-west towards the river Ouse. That part of the fortress which lay in front of the *principia* was known as the *praetentura*, the areas on either side of the *principia* were known as *latera praetorii* and the part behind the *principia* was known as the *retentura*.

Having decided on orientation, the surveyors' next task was to mark out the line enclosing the interior space and dividing it from the defences. It is likely that the work was set in train by placing the *groma* at the intended intersection of the two main streets, the *via principalis*, which ran across the front of the headquarters building to join the two side gates (at York it ran north-west/south-east), and the *via praetoria* which joined the headquarters to the main gate or *porta praetoria* (at York the street ran north-east/south-west). Before work began in earnest an appropriate sacrifice was probably made at a temporary altar set up at the intersection to invite the gods to look favourably on the fortress and its future occupants.

At York the intended dimensions of the space within the defences appears to have been 1,600pM (473.6m) north-east/south-west by 1,360pM (402.56m) north-west/south-east. These dimensions were probably chosen to allow for easy setting-out and internal subdivision without the need for complex measuring and surveying exercises. Whilst the surveyors who drew up

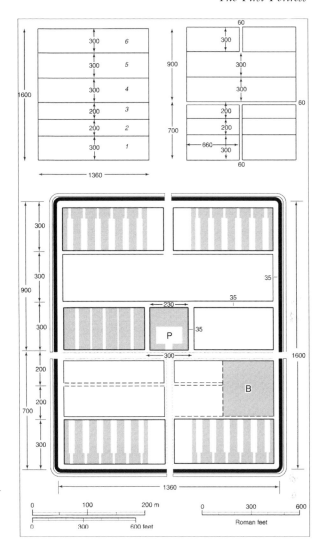

14 A theoretical reconstruction of the late first-century fortress plan showing the principal measurements in Roman feet. *P* = principia (headquarters building), *B* = baths

the plan were highly trained specialists, the legionaries who had to execute it may not have had numeracy skills of a high order. They therefore had to have a plan which could easily be checked for accuracy.

An advantage of a length of 1,600pM combined with a width of 1,360pM is that it helps overcome one of the biggest problems encountered in surveying a large and somewhat uneven site with simple instruments, namely getting the corners at as near to right angles as possible. It is at this point that we see the value of Pythagoras's theorem, clearly well known to the Roman army, which states that in a right-angled triangle the square of the hypotenuse equals the sum of the square of the other two sides. A site 1,600pM x 1,360pM has a hypotenuse, or diagonal, of almost exactly 2,100pM, a round number which could easily be checked during laying out to ensure that the sides were parallel and corners had right angles. 2,100 is also 60 x 35 and, as we shall see from time to time in this chapter, a 35pM unit was frequently employed in the fortress plan.

Along the north-east/south-west axis the 1,600pM dimension was sub-divided into three unequal parts: a *praetentura* of 700pM, a strip for the *latera praetorii* and *principia* of 300pM and a *retentura* of 600pM. The *praetentura* was then divided into three strips (1-3), one 300pM wide and two 200pM wide. The *retentura* was subdivided into two strips (5-6) each 300pM wide.

Once the six strips had been laid out, the next step was to lay out the spaces for the principal streets. The spaces for the *via praetoria* and its continuation to the rear of the *principia*, the *via decumana*, were probably 60pM (17.76m) wide with porticoes 10pM (2.96m) wide on each side. There are few records of the *via praetoria*, which is not surprising as much of it lies underneath modern Stonegate, but according to a sighting in 1847 it seems to have had a stone-built sewer below it like that known at the baths (see p.43 below). The *via decumana* was recorded in a basement of the Treasurer's House on Chapter House Street in 1954 where it can still be seen. This is where sightings of the ghosts of Roman soldiers have been made from time to time – thereby providing an important component of York's many 'ghost tours'! At the Treasurer's House also there is the base of a stone column, still in its original position, which supported the roof of a portico on the south-east side of the Roman street, although the fact that the base is of stone probably means it does not belong to the first fortress. A cobbled surface with a stone-lined drain alongside it, either the *via decumana* itself or part of the internal layout of the building behind the headquarters, was seen in a modern sewer repair trench in Chapter House Street in 1996.

The *via principalis*, which like the *via praetoria* was probably 60pM (17.76m) wide, was taken from the north-east side of Strip 3, and once again there was probably a portico 10pM (2.96m) wide on each side of the street. In 1998 observations made in a series of sewer repair trenches in Low Petergate, at a depth of 4.5m (14ft 9in) below modern level, recorded a hard-packed gravel surface and indications of a central gutter.

Around the perimeter of the fortress, behind the defences, there was a wide space known as the *intervallum*. This served to lessen the chance that any enemy missiles which cleared the defences would damage the buildings. The *intervallum* also accommodated a street known as the *via sagularis* (from the word *sagum*, a type of cloak often used by soldiers and made from a rectan-gular piece of cloth) which allowed troops to be moved quickly around the perimeter to any point of attack. At York the *intervallum* is known to have been 35pM (10.36m) wide in the late first century, although it was widened in the second century. Perhaps surprisingly, the *via sagularis* was not given a hard-wearing surface until the mid-second century and it seems that other spaces given over to streets, except the main ones, were not surfaced either in the early years of the fortress.

The next stage in fortress layout was the addition of the minor street spaces. Working from the south-west, the first street was taken from the south-west side of Strip 2. This was located at 9 Blake Street where it was 10pM (2.96m) wide, but again was not surfaced in the late first century. The next street which has not yet been recorded was, on metrological grounds, probably taken from the south-west side of Strip 3, but it cannot have run the whole distance from the *via praetoria* to the south-east *intervallum* because of the baths block. The *via quintana*, which is the street running north-west/south-east behind the *principia*, was recorded in the Minster excavations; it was probably 35pM (10.36m) wide and was taken out of the north-east side of Strip 4. The street between Strips 5 and 6 was located in excavations in advance of the Minster Library extension in 1997. No minor street spaces running north-east/south-west have been discovered except for that north-west of the *principia* which in excavation was found to be 35pM wide. It can be presumed that the space to the south-east was also 35pM wide.

THE LEGIONARY HEADQUARTERS

Once the basic framework of streets had been established, work could start on the construction of buildings. At the centre of the fortress was the headquarters (*principia*) where the administration of the legion took place and official religious ceremonies were observed. It existed as a courtyard with a range of buildings on each side including on one side (the north-east at York) a great aisled hall or basilica *(15-17)*. At one end of the hall there was the tribunal, a podium, from where the commanding officer addressed his troops. Behind the basilica there was a row of rooms which served as offices except for the one in the centre. This was the *aedes*, the legionary shrine in which sacred cult statues were kept along with the legion's standards when the men were not out on campaign. Below the *aedes* there was often a cellar used as a strong room for legion funds and the soldiers' pay and savings. The remains of the headquarters discovered in the Minster excavations at York were those of a stone building thought to date to about the year 100 which may have replaced an earlier timber structure.

We are used to seeing large buildings in our modern cities, but it is worth reflecting for a moment on the likely impact made by the legionary headquarters on a native inhabitant of the York region in the early second century. Even when compared with other buildings in the Roman fortress, it must have appeared extraordinary both in terms of its sheer size and in terms of its architectural ambition; nothing remotely like it had ever existed in the north of England before.

Although only parts of the basilica and offices were found in the excavations, it appears that the space for the headquarters building (including por-

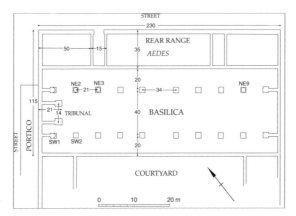

15 Conjectural plan of headquarters basilica with measurements in Roman feet (based on Phillips, D. and Heywood, B., 1995. Excavations at York Minster, 1: From Roman Fortress to Norman Cathedral: figs 4 and 7). The doorway in the north-east wall was an addition to the original plan

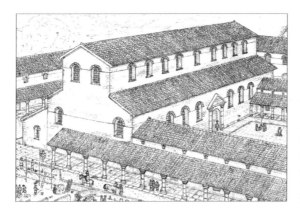

16 Reconstruction of the headquarters basilica of the Roman fortress looking east (mid-second century); the first cohort barracks under construction in stone in the foreground

ticoes to north-west and south-east) was a square of sides 265pM (78.44m) long. The basilica itself measured 230pM (68.08m) long x 110pM (32.56m) wide with the main hall 80pM (23.68m) wide, the central nave being 40pM (11.84m) wide. The height of the basilica is difficult to estimate, but 80pM (23.68m) to the top of a gabled roof is not impossible and would answer the demands of symmetry. By way of comparison the height of the nave vault in the Minster today is about 30m (98 ft), perhaps only slightly higher than the Roman building.

The evidence suggests that there were sixteen free-standing columns, a row of eight on each side, supporting the nave walls of the basilica and at each end of the rows there were probably half columns. The lower part of one free-standing column (SW2, the north-westernmost on the south-west side of the nave) can still be seen in its original position in the Minster Undercroft. A more or less complete column (NE2, the north-westernmost on the north-east side of the nave) was found in the excavations where it had fallen, perhaps in the late ninth century *(6)*. It stands about 26pM (7.7m) high and the shaft is 3pM (0.88m) in diameter at top and base, although it swells slightly in the centre. This is a device known as entasis which is intended to correct what would

17 Reconstruction of the interior
of the headquarters basilica of the
Roman fortress looking north-west
showing the north-eastern arcade and
entrance to the shrine on the right.
The arch over the tribunal at the end
of the basilica and the larger than
life-size statues are conjectural

otherwise be a visual illusion of concavity. The column, the only complete
example from a Roman basilica in Britain, has been re-erected outside the
south door of the Minster and gives some hint of the grandeur of the building
from which it comes *(colour plate 1)*.

The distance between the columns on each side of the nave, measured
centre to centre, appears to have been 21pM (6.22m) except between those in
the middle of the row where the distance must have been 34pM (10.06m). If
this is correct, then a rectangle defined by column centres in the centre of the
nave, a rectangle which one would have had to pass through on going from
the main door to the *aedes*, measured 34pM x 40pM (the width of the nave),
i.e. 1,360pM squared. This was exactly one fortieth of the area of the fortress
itself within the defences and is one indication of the care with which the plans
of the buildings of a Roman fortress were conceived and integrated with the
plan of the site as a whole.

As no legionary headquarters buildings have survived to any great extent
above ground level in Britain or elsewhere in the western Empire, it is difficult, in spite of the valuable evidence from the Minster excavations, including the complete column, to know what the York *principia* looked like in any

detail. It is not clear, for example, whether the columns supported arcades or flat lintels, although the former is assumed for the reconstruction illustration *(17)*. Stone lintels, especially for the central span of 34pM, would have required some massive blocks and a stone wall above them would surely have imposed too great a weight for the columns to bear. Any lintels are therefore likely to have been timber and the walls above them timber-framed. If the building was constructed in stone throughout then arcades are more likely.

RELIGION AND THE ARMY

The importance of the *aedes* or legionary shrine as the emotional and spiritual focus of the fortress cannot be doubted. Observation of cult practices associated with a variety of religious beliefs, some of which might appear to us more like magic or superstition, was an important part of the lives of Roman soldiers as it was of other members of the population.

There is insufficient space here to discuss in any great detail what religious beliefs the Romans held, although we shall return to the evidence from York itself in later chapters. It is clear, however, that the Romans approached such 'big questions' as the origins and destiny of humankind, and the place of the individual in the cosmos as a whole from a religious point of view. The forces that have made us what we are and those that influence what we are to become perplexed the Romans just as they continue to perplex us today in spite of the great advances in scientific and other forms of knowledge since Roman times. As far as the question of human origins is concerned, the Roman world possessed a number of creation myths, derived mostly from the Greeks. In one of them Euronyme, the goddess of all things, rose naked from Chaos, divided the sea and sky, and created the seven planetary powers with a titan and titaness ruling over each. Evidence that this account was known in York soon after the Roman conquest takes the form of two small bronze plaques found on the site of the Old Station in 1839-40, south-west of the Ouse. They carry dedications in Greek by a man named Scribonius Demetrius to, in one case, 'the gods of the military commander's residence' and in the other to 'Ocean and Tethys', a titan and titaness who ruled the goddess Venus. Demetrius has been identified as a school teacher whom the Roman author Plutarch met at Delphi in 83-4 when he heard of the man's experiences on a journey to the 'western isles' beyond the ocean encircling the civilised world.

When seeking eternal truths about humanity's place in the cosmos, the Romans turned as a matter of course to phenomena which had an unchanging or predictable quality, such as the alternation of day and night, the changing seasons, the configuration of the stars and the motions of the planets around the earth, then assumed to be the fixed centre of the universe. For this reason, heavenly bodies were a focus for religious ideas and cult practice in the Roman world. The gods and goddesses themselves were believed to be immortal and immutable beings, and seven of the more influential were identified with the planets: Jupiter, Saturn, Venus, Sol (the sun), Mercury, Mars, Luna (the moon). Their approximate distance from the earth and nature of their orbits had been established by astronomical observation over many centuries.

In addition to the planetary deities the Romans practised the cult of innumerable others, some local, some empire-wide, in their search for spiritual enlightenment. At the heart of all cult practice, however, was the idea of making a bargain with the gods which was given ritual and ceremonial form in sacrifices and offerings. Requests for divine favour might cover a wide range of topics. For soldiers, however, success in battle was no doubt important, at least at certain times, although to judge by the evidence of inscriptions, success in the hunt seems to have been equally sought after. In the daily lives of all Romans, whether soldiers or not, the fertility of crops and beasts (as well as people) was a matter frequently brought to the attention of the gods. Although the Roman world had many great cities, most people lived on the land and depended more or less entirely on the fortunes of agriculture in their immediate locality. As a result the timetable of cult practice throughout the empire was closely linked to the cycle of the seasons, and fertility deities were popular. They included the *matres*, or mother goddesses, who are named in three altar dedications from York – at least one made by a soldier (p.61) – and are also shown on a relief seated and in triplicate, as is usual, to emphasise their power.

A soldier's experience of religious observance involved cults which were officially sponsored and those which he practised unofficially on a day-to-day basis. For the observance of officially sponsored cults the fortress shrine might well have contained statues representing the three principal deities of the classical pantheon: Jupiter, Juno and Minerva. They are often known as the Capitoline Triad because of their temples on the Capitoline Hill in Rome. The members of the triad were particularly associated with the well-being and security of the empire, and dedications to Jupiter and Minerva are common in Britain, especially in military areas, although there is only one – to Jupiter - from York. This appears on the Bishophill altar (p.15) where the god is associated with 'the gods and goddesses of hospitality and home' by the dedicator, Publius Aelius Marcianus, the commander of a body of auxiliary troops.

In addition to representations of the Capitoline Triad, the legionary shrine probably housed an image of the reigning emperor and members of his family. As the empire's chief priest (*pontifex maximus*, as Trajan is described on the King's Square inscription), the emperor sought to dominate its sacred as well as its secular life. Strictly speaking, emperors were not treated as gods while living, but might be deified after their deaths. The living emperor's spirit (his *numen*) was, however, considered to have sacred power, and dedications were made to it by soldiers and civilians alike (see p.88). The cult of the emperor may be seen as Roman ancestor-worship on a grand scale, the emperor being conceived as father of his people (*pater patriae*, as he is referred to in inscriptions), and it was energetically promoted by the state because it provided a unifying spiritual and emotional focus for disparate subject people who might otherwise have little in common.

Attendance at the official ceremonies honouring the Capitoline Triad and deified emperors would have been compulsory for the soldiers. The commander would have presided as the emperor's representative and carried out important sacrifices. One aspect of the associated ceremonies was the prediction of future events and a legion would have had on its strength an *augur*, who studied the flight of birds and other natural phenomena, and a *haruspex*, who contemplated the entrails of sacrificed animals. In their own time the men were free to indulge in whatever religious practices they chose. It is, therefore, usual to find that Roman forts and fortresses were surrounded by diverse temples and altars. Deities favoured by soldiers would have included those of the classical pantheon, such as Mars and Hercules, who presided over war and combat, and also Victoria (the goddess of victory) and Fortuna (goddess of fortune or luck). In addition, the men would have worshipped deities of their homelands, of countries in which they had seen service and of the locality in which they presently found themselves, often described simply as the *genius loci* (spirit of the place).

FORTRESS BUILDINGS

We may return now to the buildings of the fortress and move across the *via quintana* from the headquarters basilica. The south-west corner of a building seen in the Minster excavations should probably be identified as part of the commanding officer's house (*praetorium*). This would have approximated in plan and appointments to a luxurious town house with a central courtyard and garden surrounded by ranges of rooms, many of them heated. Although some parts were used for official business, the private rooms may be envisaged as something of an island of domestic tranquility in the bustling military world.

Other major buildings in the fortress would have included granaries, workshops and a hospital, but at York the only other facility about which anything is known is the bath house. Baths were a vital part of Roman life not only for washing, but also for a range of social activities; in modern municipal parlance they functioned as a 'leisure centre'. As a result the baths needed a large area, so large in fact that, although fortresses had sufficient space to accommodate them within the defences, fort bath houses were usually placed outside the gates. At York the bath house plot was located on the south-east side of the *praetentura* and occupied about 9,100 square metres (10,900 square yards).

Because they needed heat and water, bath houses had to be constructed

18 Peter Addyman (former Director of York Archaeological Trust) inspects the main channel of the Roman sewer which served the legionary fortress baths at the Church Street site, 1972

largely of stone even if other fortress buildings used timber. The presence of a late first-century stone structure at York was demonstrated in excavations in 1991 at 12-18 Swinegate, although few details of its plan were revealed. The most spectacular discovery in the fortress baths had, however, been made in 1972 when the main sewer was located on the north side of Church Street *(18)*. The principal channel, fed by a number of side channels, was found running for some 44m (144ft) on a north-west/south-east line to a point close to the edge of the south-eastern *intervallum*, where it returned to the north-east.

The sewer was constructed from massive blocks of millstone grit and limestone, and was large enough for a person of average height to crawl along – in Roman times slaves would have been sent down to clean it out. In places there were round arches above the main channel, which presumably supported walls in the building above. The sewer's function was to remove water and other waste from the baths and latrines, and its size indicates the vast quantity of water that was used when the place was going full blast. At Exeter it has been calculated that the legionary baths may have used some 318,000 litres (70,000 gallons) a day. The source of the water used in the fortress at York is difficult to determine, although some supplies may have been pumped out of wells or taken from the rivers Foss and Ouse. Another source, however, was suggested by examination of the silt deposited in the sewer which, surprisingly, produced the seeds and pollen of plants which prefer limestone subsoil. This suggests the existence of an aqueduct to bring water from the nearest limestone country, probably in the Tadcaster area some 20km (12 miles) away to the south-west or in the North York Moors to the north-east, although no trace of it has ever been found. We should not necessarily, however, be thinking in terms of a massive stone structure like the well-known aqueducts in the Mediterranean world which had to cross great valleys and gorges. Where known, aqueducts in Britain were mostly large ditches which followed the line of natural contours, the water being propelled through a ceramic or concrete pipe by the force of gravity.

The usual practice before bathing in Roman style was to work up a sweat and open the skin's pores with exercise. One then entered a hot room or *caldarium*, where after oiling the body, sweat and dirt were removed with a form of metal scraper known as a *strigil*. The *caldarium* was heated by what is known as a hypocaust system in which hot air circulated below a floor raised on pillars (*pilae*) and might also be sent up the walls in hollow ceramic flues. Part of the York fortress baths' *caldarium* was excavated in 1930-1 and an apsed (curved) end wall and large millstone grit blocks which originally supported the floor can still be seen in a public house known, appropriately, as the Roman Bath in St Sampson's Square. A heated room was also found in Church Street where the floors had been supported on pillars of tile *(19)*. Other rooms in the baths, the locations of which are not known at York, would have included another hot room to provide the dry heat of a sauna, and a *frigidarium* with a cold bath into which one plunged so as to close up the pores after bathing. A massage with aromatic oils might follow to complete the experience.

Bone and pottery counters from the silt in the sewer suggest that, in addition to bathing, a popular activity in the baths was the playing of and, doubt-

19 Church Street (1972): a heated room in the fortress baths with tile pilae from a hypocaust system

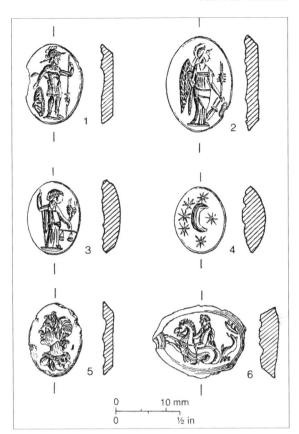

20 Intaglios (gem stones) from the
Church Street sewer:

1 Mars
2 Fortuna
3 Aequitas (equity)
4 Moon and six stars (? representing the
  other known planets) symbols of the
  heavens, home of Jupiter
5 Maenad, a female participant in the
  cult of Bacchus
6 Cupid on a hippocamp – symbolising
  the soul's journey to the Isles of the
  Blessed

less, gambling on board games such as *ludus duodecim scriptorum*, a form of
backgammon, and *ludus latrunculorum*, a form of chess. Personal items found
included two gold pendants *(colour plate 4)* which had probably been worn as
amulets or charms, and a number of intaglios, the carved gemstones used in
seal rings, bearing incised representations of deities such as Mars, Roma and
Fortuna, appropriate to the soldier and his world *(20)*.

More robust entertainments than those possible in the baths would have
been on offer in an amphitheatre, and a slip of bone bearing the inscription
DOMINE VICTOR VINCAS FELIX ('Lord Victor may you have a lucky
win') found on the chest of a body in a Roman coffin, hints that gladiators
practised their bloodthirsty skills in York. However, in contrast to the other
two permanent fortresses in Britain, Chester and Caerleon, no amphitheatre
has yet been found adjacent to the fortress at York, although speculation as to
its location will continue.

This survey of the buildings of the early fortress can be concluded with a brief
look at the soldiers' living accommodation. Excavations at 9 Blake Street in the
praetentura revealed the remains of what may have been a self-contained residential block, although for whom is not clear *(21)*. There were two episodes of

timber building; the first of the late first century and the second a reconstruction of perhaps the early second century. The buildings were identified from a series of shallow slots. These slots had once held timber beams into which uprights were morticed at intervals. By analogy with fortress buildings elsewhere, the walls between the uprights were probably made of wattles, trimmed wooden rods, which were plastered with clay, or daub as it is usually known. No timber survived on the site and it had probably been carefully removed when the buildings were rebuilt in stone in the mid-second century. The building plan consisted of two ranges of rooms, with their longer axes on a north-west/south-east alignment, separated by a small alley. As will become clearer when we look at the stone buildings which replaced them (p.76-8), the north-east range probably contained living quarters and the south-west range a kitchen, identified primarily by the presence of hearths, presumably for cooking. A remarkable component of the finds associated with the timber buildings was a collection of ten pottery lamps which came from an area immediately to the north-west of the residential range *(22)*. Lamps were often used in Roman religious ritual and so there may have been some sort of shrine in the vicinity.

The long barrack blocks in which the ordinary soldiers lived were placed around the perimeter of a fortress (i.e. on the south-west side of the *praetentura* and north-east side of the *retentura*). In addition, the barracks of the first cohort were located alongside (at York to the north-west of) the *principia* and parts of two blocks were found in the Minster excavations. Each ordinary barrack block housed a century and normally consisted of ten pairs of rooms, each pair accommodating eight men. At the end of a block nearest the defences there was a suite of rooms for the centurion and his family. Very little is known of the late first to

21 Remains of timber buildings in the legionary fortress at 9 Blake Street showing beam slots and post-holes (looking south-west; 2m scale)

22 Two pottery lamps from the early
second-century buildings at 9 Blake
Street (length *c.*70mm)

early second-century timber barracks at York, although remains – largely beam
slots and post-holes – have been found in the Aldwark-Bedern area near the east
corner (Sites 2-3, 7-8 on *13*), at the Minster Library, and at 9 Blake Street next
door to the building described above. It is possible to estimate that each barrack
block was 265pM (78.5m) long and a pair, including the alley between them, was
85pM (25m) wide. Few remains of the timber barracks of the first cohort were
found, but if the stone versions of the mid-second century had much the same
overall dimensions, then each block was about twice the width (about 21m/69ft)
of the ordinary barracks. Little is known of the internal appointments of York's
barracks, but from excavated debris we know the walls were usually plastered and
given simple painted designs based on red stripes. A fragment of lead pipe found
in what was probably a centurion's quarters at 1-5 Aldwark suggests it had a water
supply.

THE LATE FIRST–CENTURY DEFENCES

The fortress defences present the archaeologist with some of Roman York's
most difficult problems. Although they have been extensively studied, notably
by Wellbeloved in the 1840s, Miller in the 1920s, and York Archaeological
Trust at regular intervals since 1972, many uncertainties regarding the
sequence of construction remain (see also p.67-75). It is clear, however, that
the earliest fortress defences consisted, first of all, of a ditch and behind it a

rampart *(23)*. Excavations at Interval Towers SW5 and SW6 have shown that the ditch was re-cut on a number of occasions (see p.74), but that in origin it was of a typical military form with flat-bottomed slot at the base. This slot is sometimes referred to as an 'ankle-breaker', but in addition to its defensive role, it allowed the ditch to be cleaned out easily by running a spade along the base. An open space, the berm, separated the ditch from the rampart.

Construction of the rampart at York was begun by the placing of timbers, probably oak logs, on the ground surface to create a stable base. The rampart was then built up to a height of at least 3m (9ft) and width of approximately 6m (19ft) using material dug out of the ditch, strengthened with timber strapping and bands of turf; the outer faces were also composed of turf. At the rear the base was vertical for about 1m (3ft 3in). Steps were presumably placed at intervals around the defences to allow access to a timber walkway about 2.5m (8ft) wide along the top of the rampart which was protected by a timber palisade. At intervals around the circuit there were timber towers, post-holes for which have been found at two sites on the south-west side of the fortress. The four gates would also have been of timber, but no remains of them have been found.

A FORTRESS ANNEXE?

It was suggested by RCHME that outside the defences of the fortress on its north-west side there was a defended subsidiary enclosure or annexe in an area which in post-Roman times was occupied by the seat of the Anglo-Saxon Earl of Northumbria (the 'Earlsburgh') and after the Norman Conquest by St Mary's Abbey. In excavations in the abbey grounds from 1952-7 (which unfortunately remain unpublished except in summary form) a substantial

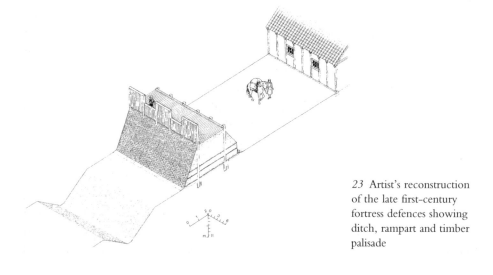

23 Artist's reconstruction of the late first-century fortress defences showing ditch, rampart and timber palisade

Roman stone wall was found under the south wall of the south aisle of the abbey church. The Roman wall continued to the north-west the line of the south-west defences of the fortress. This wall was interpreted as part of an annexe defence. On the north-west side of the proposed enclosure a stone wall was found in the nineteenth century in two places in Marygate, on much the same line as the fourteenth-century abbey defences. However, this is probably the same wall as was recorded in Marygate in 1997 which appeared to be twelfth-century and not Roman. For the time being therefore, the annexe idea can probably be dismissed. Having said this, the 1950s excavations did produce a few pieces of mid-first century glass and pottery which are unusual in a York context and may indicate early Roman activity in this area.

THE LEGION AND ITS ROADS

Although based in York, the Ninth Legion would have spent a good deal of its time on campaign, especially, perhaps, during the governorship of Agricola (c.78-84) when the north-west of England and much of Scotland were conquered. In addition to fighting, a vital part of the work of conquest was fort building and road construction. The Roman army's usual method of pacifying conquered territory was to establish a network of forts connected by roads; this broke up potentially hostile people into small groups and prevented them coming together as a large army. These roads are, of course, the stuff of myth and legend, especially as regards their straightness. When looked at in detail, however, Roman roads were not always as straight as we suppose, although they often incorporated long straight stretches since their main purpose was to get the army from A to B as quickly as possible. Furthermore, the military surveyors had no need to worry about routing roads around anyone's property as Roman rule was absolute.

The lines of the major Roman approach roads to York are fairly well known, in general terms if not in detail, and are often preserved in modern roads and other topographical features. One of the earliest Roman roads to York followed the route usually believed to have been taken by the Ninth Legion on its initial advance into the region. This was a continuation of what is now known as Ermine Street, which ran north from London to Lincoln and then on to a crossing over the river Humber near Wintringham. On the north side of the Humber the road – now known as Humber Street – ran from a fort at Brough-on-Humber to another at Hayton near Market Weighton, about 25km (15 miles) south-east of York. The road then approached York from the east. Another important approach road from the south, the Roman equivalent of the A1, came north via forts at Doncaster (*Danum*), Castleford (*Lagentium*) and Tadcaster (*Calcaria* – 'limestone quarries'). From Tadcaster the road ran north-eastwards to York, its line corresponding closely to the present A64 as far as Dringhouses, approximately 3.25km (2 miles) from the city centre. This was demonstrated in 2003 at the site of the former Starting Gate pub (Site 16 on *1*). North-east of Dringhouses excavations have shown that the Roman road ran a little to the north-west of what is now Tadcaster Road, Mount Vale, The Mount and Blossom Street. On a site on the north-west side of Blossom Street (at Nos 14-20; Site 13 on *1*), about 112m (120 yards) from Micklegate Bar, the road was examined archaeologically in 1953-4 and 1991 and shown to be composed of hard-packed gravel and about 10m (33ft) wide, very substantial in York terms. There remains some doubt, however, as to how this road continued to the north-east from Blossom Street as can be seen on *1*; it does not appear possible to join it up in a straight line with another equally substantial Roman road, also running on a north-east/south-west alignment, apparently located at Micklegate Bar, but certainly located at sites in Micklegate and Tanner Row *(44)*, and fully excavated in 1988 at Wellington Row close to the river crossing *(25, 45)*. Only further archaeological work can resolve this problem.

In the excavations at Wellington Row trenches were dug through the complete thickness of road make-up, revealing some 4m (13ft) of superimposed surfaces, the latest lying just below modern ground level. Below the earliest road there were layers of turf and a spread of hazel branches, many of them bearing nuts. At first it was thought that this material was ground preparation for the road, a way of creating a stable base on soft ground, but while the turf may have had this function, the branches bear no comparison to the sturdy wattle and timber work used as a base for Roman roads elsewhere. Instead it is suggested that the hazel branches, below which a wooden bowl made of alder was also found *(24)*, had a religious significance and formed an offering to the local deities for the good fortune of those using the road. The hazel may have grown in one of the sacred groves favoured by native British religion and the nuts had, perhaps, a particular significance as symbols of fruitfulness. The bowl and branches are therefore a good example of a votive foundation deposit of the kind which is common in the Roman world and occurs in other contexts at York.

The first gravel surface make-up at Wellington Row was about 10m (33ft) wide with a camber to allow drainage on each side. The fact that this road sloped gently down towards the river suggests that the crossing was by ferry rather than a bridge at this time. It is even possible that at low tide the river was fordable. At all events, a bridge would not have been feasible given the difference between the levels on the opposing river banks. Overlying the earliest road surface was a deposit of clean silt, clearly deposited by water and probably the result of a flood. Although York has become well known for its floods in recent years, this is the only archaeological evidence for a flood of Roman date yet found. The Romans may have been taken by surprise by the rising waters, but their response was to build up the road level by about 1m (3ft 3in) with a mound (*agger*) of large cobbles which was then covered by layers of fine, hard-packed gravel *(25)*.

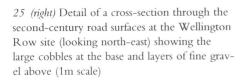

24 *(above)* Wooden bowl found underneath the earliest Roman road at Wellington Row site (0.20m scale)

25 *(right)* Detail of a cross-section through the second-century road surfaces at the Wellington Row site (looking north-east) showing the large cobbles at the base and layers of fine gravel above (1m scale)

There is insufficient space here to discuss the other Roman roads around York in any detail, although it may be noted that present-day streets Bootham and Clifton are on the line of a road which headed north-west from the fortress's north-west gate (*porta principalis dextra*) to Catterick (*Cataractonium*) and ultimately the northern frontier of *Britannia*. In addition, another important road heading north-eastwards emerged from the north-east gate (*porta decumana*). It has been found at sites in the Groves area of the city and, after crossing the river Foss, probably ran through what is now Heworth Golf Course before taking the line now followed by the Malton Road and making for Malton (*Derventio*) itself, 27km (17 miles) from York, where there was a Roman fort founded in the late first century. A route to the Roman town at Aldborough (*Isurium Brigantum*) is probably represented by a road recorded about 2km west of the centre of York in the Severus Hills area. It was once thought to join a road which branched off the main road from the south-west at 14-20 Blossom Street (Site 13 on *1*), but recent research suggests this is unlikely.

ROMAN CAMPS

In 2002 two Roman camps were discovered by aerial photography at Monk's Cross, some 5km (3 miles) north-east of York city centre *(26)*, one of which has been almost completely excavated. The camps are some 400m (440 yards) north-west of the line proposed above for the road to Malton and aligned on

26 Aerial view (looking east) of a Roman camp rampart at Monk's Cross about 5km (3 miles) north-east of York, revealed as a soil mark after ploughing

it. 'Seven or eight' Roman camps in the York area were recorded by the anti-quarians William Stukeley and Francis Drake in the eighteenth century, but at locations not exactly stated, although it must be likely that the Monk's Cross camps and another pair on Bootham Stray, about 3km (2 miles) north of York, were amongst those referred to. They were presumably recognisable by the survival of their ramparts and that of the unexcavated Monk's Cross camp can still be picked out in a field to the west of the Ryedale Stadium.

All four camps have the characteristic playing-card shaped plan typical of Roman fortifications and occupy an area of some 1.25ha (3 acres). Excavations have shown that the camp defences were simple in form, consisting firstly of a ditch about 1m (3ft 3in) wide and about 0.75m (2ft 6in) deep, and secondly of a rampart largely composed of the clay dug out of the ditch and strengthened with turf. Entrances existed on each side; at Bootham Stray they are defended by *claviculae*, extensions to the defences turned inwards and outwards across the openings to prevent a frontal assault. The camp excavated at Monk's Cross had *tituli*, short lengths of ditch in front of the gate openings which served the same purpose. Within this camp no ancient features were identified and the soldiers presumably lived in tents which have left no trace. On abandonment, it appears that the camp ramparts were partly demolished and pushed back into the ditches.

The excavated camp at Monk's Cross appears, on the basis of pottery found in its ditch, to date to about the time of the reign of the emperor Hadrian (117-38), although it is not known if the other camps are contemporary. Their form and dimensions suggest, however, that they are late first- to early second-century. The purpose of these camps remains uncertain, but one possibility is that they were created as part of military training exercises and should there-fore be described as 'practice camps'. Alternatively, they may have had some strategic role in local military arrangements for the defence of York.

THE LEGION AND ITS SUPPLIES

The arrival of the legion at York would have had a major impact on the local economy, creating a sudden increase in demand for a wide range of commodities, particularly building materials and foodstuffs. It is not clear how the army went about acquiring supplies in the early years of its presence in the north, but one can envisage, on the one hand, direct requisitioning from the local people and use of forced labour, and on the other, various forms of trade based on both barter and the use of coinage. In addition, a certain amount of manufacturing clearly took place in and around the fortress site. If local resources were inadequate, however, goods were brought in from elsewhere.

By analogy with practice elsewhere in the empire, it is likely that the legion took a piece of land adjacent to the fortress under its direct control. This is usually referred to as a *prata* or *territorium* and was perhaps as much as 50,000ha (125,000 acres) in extent. The location and size of any York *territorium* is unknown, but its creation may, as already noted (p.29), have involved sweeping away some native settlements such as that recorded at Rawcliffe Moor. West of Tadcaster (*Calcaria*), in an area about 15km (9 miles) south-west of York, aerial photography by Herman Ramm for the RCHME identified a series of Roman roads running east-west, perpendicular to a major north-south road (now known as The Rudgate), which he suggested might represent Roman re-organisation of the landscape associated with the creation of a legionary *territorium*. Closer to the fortress at York, and again within any *territorium*, there would have been a zone set aside for soldiers' families to reside and for facilities such as stores and workshops for which no space existed within the defences. The evidence for this zone from which an important area of civilian settlement at York would develop will be discussed in Chapter 4.

The *territorium* would have been used for a number of supply purposes including the collection of timber and extraction of stone suitable for building purposes. As far as stone is concerned, no certain Roman quarries can be located today, but two types used from the late first century onwards can be found no more than 30km (19 miles) west of York. Millstone grit, a coarse sandstone usually in the form of massive blocks, was employed in monumental structures such as the bath house sewer (described above), where its load-bearing properties were of particular value. Millstone grit was also, surprisingly perhaps, frequently used for sculpture, especially tombstones *(colour plate 10)*. Equally popular for building and sculpture was magnesian limestone from the quarries in the Tadcaster area. This is a high-quality freestone; in other words it has no distinct bedding plane and can be cut in any direction. In the facing of Roman walls it usually occurs as small blocks, and these can still be seen in surviving stretches of the fortress defences *(colour plates 3 and 6)*. A second type of limestone used in Roman York, although more often in the civilian settlements than in the fortress, is Jurassic oolite, which does have a distinct bedding plane and, as a result, is usually found as thin flat slabs. It may have come principally from the North York Moors, although a belt runs through east Yorkshire and reappears in the Lincolnshire Wolds south of the Humber. From further afield comes what we now know as 'York Stone', but is known to geologists as Elland Flag, a sandstone usually found in thin slabs and quarried in the Bradford-Huddersfield area of west Yorkshire. Finally, the ubiquitous cobbles found in Roman York, often mixed with clay to make wall foundations, may also be counted as imported stones, although they had not travelled far. While small pebbles might originate in the river beds, the cobbles, which can be up to 0.50m (20in) and more in diameter, were created during the last glaciation and were probably dug out of the moraine a short distance from the city centre.

Transporting vast quantities of stone to the fortress obviously posed a major logistical problem, but presumably rivers were used, rather than roads, whenever possible. Both millstone grit and magnesian limestone could have been shipped down the river Wharfe from quarries in the Wetherby and Tadcaster areas respectively, as far as Cawood, about 15km (10 miles) south of York, and then taken up the Ouse. Oolitic limestone may have been shipped from the Roman settlement at Malton down the river Derwent to Stamford Bridge before being transported over land to York or alternatively to its junction with the Ouse near Selby.

As well as being a source of building materials, the other principal function of the legionary *territorium* was the provision of food, both for animals and people. Grazing was required for the horses belonging to the cavalry, and the mules and oxen used for transport. Arable agriculture would have provided the grain for bread and other cereal-based foods which were staples of the army diet. In certain circumstances the soldiers may have carried out farming tasks such as harvesting and hay-making themselves.

In the early years of the Roman period sufficient food may not always have been available locally and was therefore brought from southern Britain or even further afield. A large quantity of cereal grain, probably brought to York by ship, was found in the remains of what was interpreted as a late first-century warehouse on the 39-41 Coney Street site a little to the south of the fortress on the north-east bank of the Ouse (Site 6 on *1*). On the basis of surviving beam slots it was evident that there had been two phases of timber structure. In deposits associated with the earlier building remains there were some cereal grains, but more remarkable was the large quantity of well-preserved grain beetles. An uncontrollable infestation had probably led to demolition of the building, after which the ground was sealed with a thick layer of clay before a new building was erected in its place. In the beam slots of the second phase a large amount of charred grain was found. This probably indicates an accidental fire of the sort for which there is also evidence in the civilian settlements (p.98-9). Apart from this grain we have little direct evidence for what the soldiers at York ate because refuse tips are rarely found in fortress excavations, but at 9 Blake Street such animal bones as did come to light suggested the consumption of smoked or salted shoulders of beef.

Trade with local farmers is difficult to trace archaeologically, but Rick Jones has suggested that at Naburn (p.27-9) it did not begin immediately the legion arrived as no Roman pottery from the site can be dated to before the early second century. This corresponds to evidence from elsewhere in the York region where, measured by the occurrence of material culture, not only pottery but also coinage and metalwork, the conquest appears, on the whole, to have had little immediate impact. However, in areas where communications were presumably good, such as the Vale of York, Vale of Pickering and more accessible parts of the Wolds, Roman artefacts became widely available within 50 years or so of the conquest, especially on sites near roads. In upland zones like the Pennine Dales and North York Moors the Roman conquest barely registered in the artefactual record until the third or fourth centuries.

While the bulk of their food presumably became, in due course, available in the locality, the soldiers would have been unwilling to forego their olive oil and wine which had to be imported from Mediterranean lands. Supplies arrived in large earthenware jars known as amphorae, of which numerous pieces have been found in York. The oil came largely from southern Spain and the wine from southern Gaul; the Rhône valley where Lucius Duccius Rufinus the standard-bearer had grown up, being a principal source of supply.

When local resources failed, the legionaries could not only import what they required, as in the case of foodstuffs, but they could also make things themselves. A good example of a commodity manufactured by the army is pottery *(colour plate 5)*. Although native people in the York area did make pottery, it was not of good quality and their only product was cooking vessels. The legionaries required large quantities of pottery, however, to suit their sophisticated ways of dining and food preparation. They used a wide range of vessels including bowls, platters and storage jars as well as flagons for the wine and olive oil. While the potters *(figuli)* of each legion in Britain had a distinctive style, their products were usually made in red earthenware and included a number of standard forms. Kiln waste, ash and pottery wasters (damaged and distorted vessels) have been found on sites immediately east of the fortress in the Aldwark and Peasholme Green area. In view of the prevailing wind from the south-west it was ideal for an activity like making pots and ceramic roof tiles, which produces copious smoke and noxious fumes. From material collected in recent excavations, Vivien Swan has identified three episodes of production of what has come to be known as 'Ebor ware': the first in the late first to early second century, the second in the second quarter of the second century and the third in the early third century (p.80-1). Evidence for production, largely in the second century, has also been recorded at Appletree Farm, Heworth about 3km (2 miles) east of the fortress close to a Roman road approaching York from Stamford Bridge.

Local supplies of pottery were supplemented by imports from elsewhere in Britain and from across the sea. For the most part, continental imports took the form of the shiny red tableware known as samian which was produced in

27 Helmet cheek-piece made of copper alloy, probably second century, found in barrack buildings at Purey Cust Nursing Home

Gaul. Supplies until about the year 110 came largely from an area north-east of Toulouse in the south, but after this samian came from central Gaul in the region of what is now Clermont-Ferrand and finally in the late second to early third century samian was to come from the Trier region in eastern Gaul. In addition to samian pottery, glass vessels, of which fragments have been found in some quantity in the fortress, were imported. At first glass was imported from Italy and Gaul, but also from the Rhineland and, in due course, from workshops in London. By the third century it was apparently made in York itself, the evidence being a number of ceramic vessels used for melting glass from excavations at 16-22 Coppergate, south-east of the fortress (No. 10 on *1*). Glass vessels were primarily tableware such as bowls, jars and bottles, but small phials for scented water or other cosmetics are common on military sites including York. One cannot escape the conclusion that on some occasions, Roman soldiers were pleasantly sweet-smelling!

Another group of technical specialists on the legion's staff was the smiths who worked in iron and other metals, and would have made and serviced weaponry and armour. Unfortunately very little military equipment has been found at York, although a fine copper alloy helmet cheek piece from the barracks at Purey Cust Nursing Home (Site 10 on *13*), probably of second-century date, may be a local product *(27)*. In addition, the smiths would have produced large numbers of nails and other structural fittings for the buildings. At 9 Blake Street, for example, nails occurred in some quantity in mid-second century deposits and had presumably been discarded when the timber buildings were replaced in stone. This is one of the most archaeologically visible changes which occurred in the second-century fortress as will be seen in the next chapter.

CHAPTER 3

THE FORTRESS REBUILT

Many readers will be familiar with the historical novels of Rosemary Sutcliff and, in particular, *The Eagle of the Ninth*. This tells the story of a boy who went into the wilds of Scotland to search for the truth about the unexplained disappearance of the Ninth Legion and to recover the sacred eagle standards of the cohort commanded by his father. Until relatively recently the mystery had some substance to it since there was little evidence for the fate of the legion after the years 107–8, the date of the great commemorative inscription from King's Square *(4)*. It was clear, none the less, that the Ninth Legion had departed from York before the arrival of the Sixth Legion in about the year 120. Since Rosemary Sutcliff published her book in 1954 it has become clear that the Ninth was still in existence after 120. Some scholars believe it may have been briefly based in Carlisle in the early 120s and was responsible for building the western part of Hadrian's Wall (the so-called 'Turf Wall'). Whether or not this is the case, after leaving Britain, the Ninth was probably based at Nijmegen (today in the Netherlands) in the Roman province of Lower Germany, where a few of its stamped tiles have been found. Subsequently, the legion may have been posted to the eastern empire and destroyed during a war against the Parthians in 161.

Hadrian visited Britain in the year 120 and set about securing its northern frontier with the wall which bears his name. Much of the Sixth Legion was probably sent direct to the Wall zone leaving only a small garrison to move into York. Inscriptions tell us that the legion was not only occupied on Hadrian's Wall, but also, some years later, on the Antonine Wall, the Roman frontier in Scotland between the Forth and the Clyde. This was established by the emperor Antoninus Pius in about 141 and maintained for perhaps 15-20 years. It was once thought that evidence for reconstruction in the forts on the Antonine Wall supported the idea of a revolt by the Brigantes in the middle of the second century, which is implied by an enigmatic passage in the works of the Greek writer Pausanias, but this is now deemed very unlikely.

By the time it arrived in Britain the Sixth Legion, which bore the title *victrix* meaning conqueror, had had a long and glorious history going back to Julius Caesar's time in the mid-first century BC when it had served in the Gallic Wars. Some hundred years later in AD 68 the legion was in Spain. Subsequently it was transferred to the fortress at Neuss in Germany under Quintus Petilius Cerialis, who we have already met in his role as commander of the Ninth Legion at York in 71. In 89, after supporting the emperor Domitian against the revolt of Saturninus, a legionary commander in Germany, the Sixth Legion acquired the additional title *pia fidelis* (pious and faithful) which appears as PF along with VIC for *victrix* on many of the tiles from its York workshop. The emblem of the legion was a bull. The exploits of the legion were doubtless handed down from generation to generation of soldiers and kept alive by those at York, a few of whom we know by name from inscriptions.

ROMAN INSCRIPTIONS AND ROMAN NAMES

Before meeting some of the men of the Sixth, this is an appropriate point to look at aspects of Roman monumental inscriptions since, they make up an important body of evidence for Roman York. First of all, inscriptions on stone are for the most part relatively restricted in their subject matter, being principally commemorations of public works and military success or funerary and religious dedications. They are also fairly standardised in terms of the type of information they convey. In officially inspired inscriptions, as in the case of the King's Square tablet *(4)*, the emperor and his titles feature very prominently. Inscriptions from privately sponsored buildings or monuments, such as a tablet from Clementhorpe (p.116), usually emphasise the status and achievements of the individual responsible. The lack of variety in subject matter and content allowed the employment of many stock words or phrases. Since everyone who mattered would know what these were, inscriptions were, if only to save space, often radically abbreviated so that to a modern eye most are in a sort of code. Examples of abbreviations on York inscriptions include the obvious LEG for legion and AVG for Augustus (emperor). In addition we find DM on many tombstones and sarcophagi standing for *dis manibus* meaning 'to the spirits of the dead'. On altars such as that dedicated to the *genius loci* found on the site of the railway station in York, the last line is often the formula VSLM. This means *votum solvit libens merito* which may be translated as 'willingly and deservedly paid his vow' – presumably after the god had provided what was requested.

 Abbreviation was also applied to names, but the complete form is usually readily apparent. A male citizen had the right to possess the *tria nomina* (three names) which consisted of a *praenomen* or personal name, a *nomen* or *nomen gentilicium*, a family name and a *cognomen* or private name. A good example of the *tria nomina* from York are those of the standard-bearer Lucius Duccius Rufinus *(2)*. As there were relatively few *praenomina*, they were usually abbreviated to one or two letters: L for Lucius and TI for Tiberius, for example. This lack of variety also meant that as time went on the *praenomen* was gradually dropped as it was not very useful for distinguishing between individuals and by the second century appears rarely, although it did not disappear entirely even by the third century. On York inscriptions, however, it is most common to find just two names, the *nomen* and the *cognomen*.

Female citizens usually had two names – Julia Brica on a tombstone from York is typical *(72)* – consisting of the family name in the female form, which did not change when she married, followed by the private one. The latter often bore a close resemblance to that of the woman's father. The daughter of Julia Brica was, for example, named Sempronia Martina after her father Sempronius Martinus, also referred to on the tombstone. Non–citizens and slaves are rarely mentioned in inscriptions, but were usually given just one name, sometimes with a reference to whose son or daughter they were.

While Roman names can tell us a certain amount about a person's social status, they may also convey other information, including the time when the family received citizenship. On becoming a citizen a man would often take the *nomen* of the reigning emperor, as it were in gratitude for his advancement. In Britain Flavius (and Flavia) and Aelius (and Aelia) were common, being the *nomina* respectively of the Flavian emperors (Vespasian, Titus and Domitian) and of Hadrian. Particularly common, however, was Aurelius (and Aurelia) the *nomen* of the emperor Caracalla (211-17) who granted citizenship to all free-born (i.e. non-slave) inhabitants of the empire. To some extent this was a recognition that citizenship had become so widespread that it no longer counted as a meaningful privilege, but it also allowed the state to levy more taxes as citizens paid more than non-citizens. Finally, a Roman name can indicate an individual's regional origins, even if it has been Latinised. For example, the *cognomina* of Julia Brica and Candida Barita named on tombstones from York, are thought to be native British in origin. It is possible that the pair were married to legionary veterans who had found them as attractive as a British girl named Claudia Rufina encountered in Rome by the poet Martial who wrote:

> Though brought up among the sky-blue Britons,
> She has the spirit of the latin race.

(The reference to blue is an echo of Julius Caesar's aside that the Britons painted themselves blue with woad.)

Of the men who commanded the Sixth Legion, only three are known by name from inscriptions in Britain, although the post-holder probably changed every three years or so. Two of the commanders are named on inscriptions from York itself and one on an inscription on Hadrian's Wall. Of the two from York, one was named Quintus Antonius Isauricus and he is referred to on an altar dedicated to the goddess Fortuna by his wife Sosia Juncina. This was found on the site of the baths in the north-west part of the civilian town south-west of the Ouse. The inscription is of interest not only because of the legate's name and the dedication – entirely appropriate for a soldier's wife – but because it is a relatively rare example of an altar set up by a woman. In a society where men dominated public life there were few women, other than those of Sosia Juncina's elevated status, who were able to breach the male preserve of sponsoring stone monuments.

The second legate known from York is Claudius Hieronymianus, whose name appears on the inscribed tablet commemorating his foundation of a temple of Serapis (see p.114), also located south-west of the Ouse *(3)*. The commander from the Wall gloried in the name Lucius Junius Victorinus Flavius Caelianus; he is known from an altar on which he gives thanks for military success beyond the frontier. If we now work our way down through the ranks of the Sixth Legion named on York inscriptions we come first to the camp prefect Antonius Gargilianus, a man of equestrian rank whose tombstone was found at the Minster where it had been re-used as an Anglo-Saxon grave cover. From the less elevated levels of legionary society we know of several centurions including Aurelius Super, whose sarcophagus was commissioned by his widow Aurelia Censorina *(28)*. Their names suggest membership of a family which had acquired citizenship under Caracalla. It is likely that the man had been a non-citizen recruit to the legion at a time when the social distinction between legionaries and auxiliaries was breaking down, and local recruiting for all branches of the armed services was becoming the norm.

28 Inscribed panel on the stone sarcophagus of the centurion Aurelius Super who lived for 38 years, 4 months and 13 days – QVI VIXIT AN(N)IS XXXVIII M(ENSES) III D(IES) XIII. The coffin was put in place by his wife Aurelia Censorina – AVRELIA CENSORINA CONIVNX MEMORIAM POSVIT. Found in Castle Yard in 1835

29 Altar dedicated to the Mother
Goddesses of Africa, Italy and Gaul by
Marcus Minucius Mudenus, a gubernator
(river pilot) of the Sixth Legion (height:
0.25m). Found in Micklegate in 1752

Of particular interest for the light it casts on the communications between
the Sixth Legion and the rest of the Roman world is an altar set up by
Marcus Minucius Mudenus, who refers to himself as a *gubernator* or river pilot
(29). He presumably assisted ships bringing supplies and troops up the Ouse.
The diverse origins of these vessels are hinted at by the dedication to the
'Mother Goddesses of Africa, Italy and Gaul'. Finally in this journey through
the ranks we may note the tombstone of a serving legionary named Lucius
Bebius Crescens, who is a good example of a recruit from a province cre-
ated, like Britain, late in the Roman era of expansion. He came from *Augusta
Vindelicorum* (Augsburg), a *colonia* and the capital of the province of Raetia
close to the German frontier. He died aged 43 after 23 years' service.

REBUILDING AND REPLANNING THE FORTRESS: THE PROBLEMS OF DATING

The second century witnessed many changes in both the overall organisation
of the fortress at York and the form of individual buildings, but determining
the exact historical context in which these changes took place is not an easy

matter. To some extent this is because of the inadequate records of early excavations, but a much more serious obstacle lies in the nature of archaeological evidence itself.

In the superimposed layers of building debris, refuse and so forth which make up York's archaeology there are large quantities of discarded artefacts. As far as Roman sites are concerned, by far the most numerous are pieces of broken pottery, but in addition there are objects of metal, bone, glass and other materials. The types of artefact in use and their form and composition changed over time. By studying ancient artefacts in relation to the sequences of layers in which they were found, it is possible to establish the order in which these changes occurred and create what are usually known to archaeologists as typologies. Some artefacts, notably certain types of pottery, are particularly susceptible to change. In the earlier part of the Roman period this is especially true of samian ware. In the previous chapter it was noted that samian was produced in three distinct zones in Gaul in the first to early third centuries. Individual sherds can usually be identified to a source in one of these zones, which places their date of production within a broad range, but as a result of intensive research by specialists the manufacture of many pieces can be dated to within a 10-20 year range.

In addition to pottery, coins are also potentially of great value for dating in the Roman period. Although they do not have calendar dates stamped on them as coins do today, they usually bear sufficient information to allow the date of their minting to be assigned to the reign of a particular emperor, if not to a single year in that reign. Unfortunately the quantity of Roman coin supplied to Britain, usually from mints elsewhere in the empire, varied greatly during the Roman period and so, correspondingly, does the occurrence of coins of the different emperors in archaeological contexts. Supply was dependent on numerous factors, including the ability of the imperial government to pay the army in Britain and the degree to which the coinage was debased during periods of inflation. No comprehensive survey of Roman coinage from York has yet been published, but it is clear from such reports as are available in print that the pattern of supply to York was similar to that for Britain as a whole, especially its urban sites. There are, for example, relatively few coins for the late first- and second-century emperors compared to the large quantities, many probably forged locally, for rulers of the so-called 'Gallic Empire' (see p.131) in the period 260-73. Coins of the emperor Constantine and his sons are also relatively numerous, whilst those of the emperor Theodosius (378 -88) are not.

While the approximate date of manufacture of certain classes of artefacts may be readily determined, the whole question of dating is complicated by the fact that, after being thrown away or lost, a particular pottery sherd or coin may have been redeposited many times before reaching its final resting place. This is especially true of somewhere like York which has been intensively occupied over many centuries. During this time the ground has been continuously dug into for pits and ditches, or scraped up for use in structures like the fortress ramparts. In any group of finds from an archaeological layer there will, therefore, usually be many of an earlier, often considerably earlier, date than the formation of the layer itself. For example, although the fortress rampart was probably reconstructed in the third quarter of the second century, associated layers contain large quantities of finds of earlier periods (see pp.74-5). In these circumstances the archaeologist's job is to spot the latest artefact, as this will give a date at or after which the layer was created. Even if numerous coins and samian fragments are found, however, the redeposition factor reduces the possibility of giving an exact date to a layer or associated structure. As far as Roman York is concerned, we are usually lucky to be confident in dating a building, road, stretch of defences etc. to within a range shorter than 20-30 years.

Considerable work in recent years has been devoted to scientific techniques which appear to offer some solution to the problem of dating and do not rely on the judgement of the archaeologist, whose typologies may have to be revised from time to time. Radiocarbon dating has received the greatest attention, but for the Roman period it cannot usually provide the degree of precision to replace typology of pottery and other artefacts, and the most useful scientific technique is dendrochronology. This involves matching the pattern of growth rings on ancient timbers, usually oak, to a master pattern or 'curve' which has initially been dated by radiocarbon or other means. The survival of suitable timbers for dendrochronology is, however, by no means common; firstly, it relies on the sort of waterlogged ground conditions which only occur in a few places in Britain, although they include parts of York. Secondly, timbers need to be of sufficient size (usually possessing at least 50 rings) to allow a pattern to be detected. Although dendrochronology has been extensively employed on Viking Age timbers from York, it has not yet been of great value for the Roman period. Some suitable structural timbers have been found, but as yet there appears to be insufficient comparative material to create a datable 'curve' for York.

In the first edition of this book I wrote that any statement about the dating of developments in either the Roman fortress or civilian settlements at York constitutes the best estimate that could be given at that time. Further work, I went on, would be sure to allow greater refinement in the future and this has proved to be the case in respect, for example, of the fortress defences (pp.74-5). No doubt any future account will introduce further revisions; indeed, it is likely that there will always be a measure of uncertainty about the date of even the major developments for which there is archaeological evidence, and relating them to such written history as we have will usually involve an element of informed speculation. In 1962 RCHME could confidently associate supposed episodes in the construction of the fortress defences with the reigns of particular Roman governors and emperors. We now know that this confidence was largely misplaced.

METHODS OF CONSTRUCTION IN STONE

The types and sources of stone used in Roman York have already been noted above (53-4), but before looking any further at the stone buildings in the fortress we should look at how the Romans went about using the material. While drystone walling is known from pre-Roman times in Britain, the mortared stone wall was an innovation of the Romans and allowed the construction of buildings of far greater architectural ambition than anything seen hitherto.

The stability of Roman stone buildings depended first of all, of course, on the quality of their foundations. In York they were usually set in trenches up to about 0.5-1m (1ft 6in-3ft) deep which was sufficient to protect them from the destructive effects of freezing and thawing in the winter. Either clay mixed with cobbles or mortar mixed with stone rubble was the usual foundation material. In addition, a very tough concrete was used in parts of the fortress wall (but is not like concrete we use today, which is made with cement).

Roman mortar and concrete were made in much the same way, the crucial ingredient being lime. This is produced by a process known as calcination, which involves heating limestone to approximately 1,000°C in a special kiln. The resulting lime is a powdery material, but water is added to form a paste known as slaked lime, which can be used for building. Both mortar and concrete used a mixture in different proportions of lime, sand and aggregate, usually cobbles and pebbles. Mortar had more sand but less aggregate and lime than concrete. Since lime was rather more expensive than the other components, there was a tendency to economise on it with the result that many Roman buildings, especially in the civilian settlements, had poorly bonded walls. The concrete in the fortress wall footings was, however, very hard indeed and has defeated modern demolition equipment on several occasions. Whilst a clay and cobble mix could be laid directly into the foundation trenches, fresh concrete or mortared rubble was in a semi-liquid form and it was poured into a timber framework, known as shuttering, within the trench to enable it to set in a tidy solid block with a smooth and level surface. On occasions marks of the shuttering planks are found on the surface of the foundations.

Roman building foundations in York often had timber piles driven into the base of the trenches to ensure the stability of the wall above. The Romans found that the subsoil under much of York was unstable sand or silty clay. Matters were probably made worse in certain river bank areas by a high water table, even though it was probably lower in Roman times than it is today. The timber piles, usually oak, can reach up to 3m (10ft) in length and 0.5m (20in) thickness, but it is more common to find them 0.5-1m (1ft 8in-3ft 4in) long and 100-200mm (4-8in) thick.

Some Roman walls in York had their lower courses made of large gritstone blocks, but the principal construction technique for stone walls, as elsewhere in Rome's north-western provinces, involved a mortared rubble core with narrow facing courses, of limestone in York's case. The usual method of wall-building was probably to proceed upwards in stages of a given height. The facing blocks were tapered to allow them to be pushed easily into place before the core set hard. To construct walls of a height greater than a person's reach scaffolding was required and this usually involved a timber framework which would be secured by the wall itself, rather than being a largely free-standing structure as it is today. By leaving out some of the facing stones, cross members could be inserted into the wall or, alternatively, poles were passed through the complete thickness of the wall to hold a scaffold framework on either side. The holes in the wall face, known as putlog holes, were sometimes filled in as the scaffolding was taken down, but were often left open to allow scaffolding to be re-erected if repairs were needed. Good examples of putlog holes in York can be seen on the inner face of the Multangular Tower *(30)*.

The Romans' use of masonry and lime mortar was accompanied by the development of protective plaster wall covering. At its simplest it usually consisted of about three coats. The first was relatively thick, typically 30-50mm (1-2in), consisting of lime and coarse sand with a roughened surface to take the second layer, a mortar using fine sand which was smoothed off to take the final layer of lime wash on which any decorative scheme was painted. To ensure against the paint fading, the basic colour scheme was usually applied when the plaster was still wet, a technique known as fresco. On occasions, however, paint was applied to dry plaster using a technique known as tempera. The paint was given adhesive qualities by mixing it with a glue made of egg white.

The evidence from York is that, for the most part, any wall decoration was simple, the commonest pattern being one or two coloured stripes on a white background. However, there is also evidence for one of the more elaborate approaches to design which involved dividing a wall into three distinct zones. The first metre or so above the floor was occupied by the so-called dado, often painted to resemble marble. Above this the central zone was usually painted with a range of *trompe l'oeil* effects suggesting recessed and moulded panels and

30 Detail of the Multangular Tower showing putlog holes and tile courses on the inner wall face

architectural features. In addition, there might be naturalistic motifs, such as flowers and animals, and mythological scenes. At the top of the wall was the frieze, again painted with a range of distinctive motifs. A tri-partite design of this type can be seen on a panel of reconstructed plaster in York Minster Undercroft, which came from a room added to the fortress basilica in the late fourth century (*colour plate 15* and see p.141). Above an elaborate marbled dado there is a series of panels interrupted by niches defined by classical columns. The frieze is also panelled and at one point there is a mask of tragedy which had probably been matched by a mask of comedy. Similar designs may have been applied to civilian houses in Roman York, including one excavated at 37 Bishophill Senior which produced fragments of plaster depicting human figures and stylised plants.

Moving from the walls to the floors, the best known type of Roman floor covering is the mosaic pavement and there are a few examples from the civilian settlements at York (pp.134-5). In the majority of cases, however, floors were made of more simple materials. The headquarters' basilica may have had a floor of stone flags, but military buildings usually had simple floors of beaten earth or clay although in better quality buildings *opus signinum* was employed. This is a form of concrete incorporating tile fragments to give it waterproof qualities. In the civilian settlements there are examples of timber floors (*48*).

The roofs of York's Roman buildings are the parts about which least is known since none, of course, survives and we are only left with the broken-up materials which are found in demolition layers. There is no evidence for the domes or vaults made of concrete which can still be seen in Mediterranean lands and some kind of timber framework would usually have been employed. In many cases they were probably based on triangular A-frames (see *42*) which in turn supported boards given a waterproof cladding. In the fortress this cladding usually took the form of clay tiles. Rows of rectangular tiles, known as *tegulae*, with flanges along their sides, were arranged such that each row overlapped the one below. The junctions between the *tegulae* were covered by tiles of semi-circular cross-section known as *imbrices* (plural of *imbrex*). At the eaves of the better class of Roman building there were sometimes small vertical tiles called antefixes which closed off the lowest *imbrices*. These antefixes often bore images of legionary emblems or of the gods (*31*). In addition to clay tiles, York excavations have also produced large numbers of thin sandstone slabs, usually of Elland Flag (see p.54), which in many cases can be identified as roofing material as they are pierced at one side to allow attachment to the roof timbers by an iron pin. Roof pitch would, as in Mediterranean countries today, have been quite low, probably about 25° from the horizontal – this is the pitch shown in the reconstruction illustrations *16* and *42*.

With this summary of construction techniques in mind we may now return to a consideration of the remains of fortress buildings on the ground and review a great rebuilding of timber structures in stone which began in the early second century, but only appears to have gathered pace in its third quarter.

31 Moulded ceramic antefix from the eaves of a
building, probably showing a deity (height c.23mm)

NEW WORK ON THE DEFENCES

Replacement of the timber structures on the fortress defences – the gates, towers and palisades - in stone appears to have begun in the early second century,
probably in the reign of the emperor Trajan (98-117), but it was not completed until perhaps the reign of Septimius Severus (193-211) or even later. This
was a massive undertaking. Based on certain assumptions about the size of the
gates and towers, it may be suggested that at least 48,000 cubic metres (63,000
cubic yards) of stone were required, weighing nearly 9,000 tons (the weight
of a cubic metre of magnesian limestone, the principal material employed, is
approximately 186kg/410lb). It is not surprising, therefore, that the work was
not all done at once. As excavation has been confined to restricted areas around
the perimeter of the fortress a complete sequence of construction eludes us,
but it seems that the earliest stone structures may have been the work of the
Ninth Legion before its departure. The structures in question include Interval
Tower NE6 and the East Corner Tower *(33)*, the remains of which are still
visible *(32)*. Elsewhere on the defences the timber structures would seem to
have survived until the mid- to late second century. The date of the two early
stone towers noted above is derived from pottery discovered in the trenches
dug through the pre-existing first-century rampart to build their walls. Interval
Tower NE6 was about 5.5m (18ft) square in plan, the corner tower was similar
in size, but was not exactly square in plan. It survives to a height of about 2m
(6ft 6in), but both towers may originally have stood to a height of 10m (33ft)
or more. Access to the towers was not possible at ground level, but only from
the top of the rampart. Even if the enemy breached the fortress defences it was
still possible, therefore, to use the towers as defensive strong points. In addi-

tion, it is possible that the south-east gate (*porta principalis sinistra*) belonged to the Trajanic period as the inscription dated to 107-8 found in King's Square is thought to have been set above the gateway to commemorate its construction *(4)*. The other gates of which stonework has been found, the *porta praetoria* and *porta principalis dextra* (but not the *porta decumana*), may be contemporary.

Another construction project using stone which appears to belong to the first quarter of the second century was the erection of buildings between the rampart (and cut into it in places) and the *intervallum* street (*via sagularis*). They were probably stores and cook houses. Roman soldiers did not dine together like their modern counterparts in a mess, but cooked for themselves in small groups. Experience had presumably shown that the safest place for cooking hearths was against the rampart, as far away from the barracks as possible, especially when they were timber buildings. Traces of *intervallum* buildings at York have been found near the *porta decumana* (Site 1 on *13*), near Aldwark (between Interval Tower NE6 and the east corner), at Interval Towers SW4 and SW5 (pre-dating the towers themselves) and in Dean's Park near Interval Tower NW5 (Site 9 on *13*).

Presumably because the legion was occupied with the construction of Hadrian's Wall there was apparently a reduced level of activity in the fortress in the second quarter of the second century, to judge by the relatively smaller quantity of pottery of this period recovered from excavations compared to that from comparable periods before and after. There was probably a break in the reconstruction of the fortress defences in stone. However, work resumed in the second or third quarter of the second century when it was accompanied by re-digging of the fortress ditch, and reconstruction and widening of the rampart behind the wall. Pottery found in the ditch fill and in the rampart provides the dating evidence.

The fortress wall varied in its appearance from one part of the circuit to another, probably reflecting construction in different periods, although by how long they were separated is not clear. Between the *porta decumana* and the east corner, and for an uncertain distance south-west of the corner, the fortress wall probably appeared as shown in *34*. This is based largely on the wall revealed in Miller's excavations at the east corner itself in the 1920s which is still visible standing to almost its full original height of 5m (16ft 6in) *(32)*. The wall, usually 1.5m (5ft) wide at the base, is up to 2.2m (7ft 3in) wide at the corner as this was a potentially weak spot. At the base are two courses of large blocks, the uppermost being chamfered on the outer face so as to create a plinth. The main body of the wall consists of a mortared rubble core with facing stones on both the outside and inside. At the top of the wall there is a cornice of flat stones which projects out from the face. It appears that during construction the front walls of the earlier corner tower and Interval Tower NE6 were taken down while the new fortress wall was built, but afterwards the towers were restored to their original height. Between the towers there

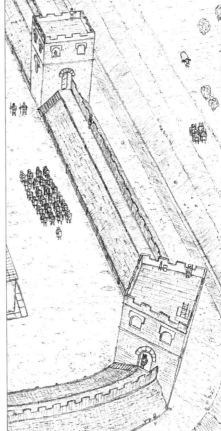

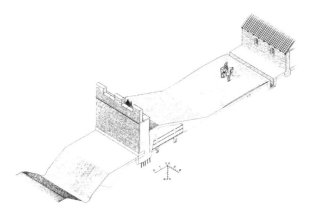

Clockwise from top left:

32 The east corner of the legendary fortress looking north-west, showing the remains of the early second-century tower and the curtain wall of the later second century

33 The process of change on the fortress defences: reconstruction drawing looking north-west, showing the east corner in the early second century with Interval Tower NE 6 (top) and the corner tower both newly built in stone set into the late first century rampart

34 Reconstruction drawing of the late second-century fortress defences immediately south-west of the east corner with a stone wall built in front of the original rampart, the rampart itself widened and the ditch dug on a new line

would probably have been a narrow parapet at the top of the wall, which has not survived, leaving behind it just enough space for a walkway.

A wall of similar form to that just described has also been found near the south corner of the fortress in a sewer trench in Parliament Street and in the basement of an adjacent property, 16 Parliament Street (*35-6*). The latter was the scene of one of the Archaeological Trust's more unusual excavations

35 The fortress wall in the basement of 16 Parliament Street (looking south-west). Basement floor level is top right (1m scale)

36 Detail of the fortress wall plinth in Parliament Street sewer trench showing stone tooling marks (0.20m scale)

which came about (in 1987) because of the need for underpinning work in the standing building. It had become unstable because one half rested on the solid fortress wall and the other half on the soft infilling of the fortress ditch. When the basement floor, itself about 2.5m (8ft) below modern ground level, was taken up, the fortress wall appeared directly underneath it. Excavation in advance of the insertion of new ground beams showed that the wall was still standing some 2m (6ft 6in) high in immaculate condition.

A wall of a rather different appearance from either of the two stretches already described existed on the south-west and north-west sides of the fortress, and also on the north-east side between the north corner and the north-east gate (*porta decumana*) and in a short stretch south-west of the south-east gate (*porta principalis sinistra*). Preservation of this wall is very good near the Multangular Tower where fine stretches near full height can be seen (*80*). Above the mortared rubble foundations there is, in contrast to the wall described above, no distinct plinth at the base of the wall, although the facing stones in the lower two or three courses of the wall are larger than those above. At the rear of the wall the face has been left roughly finished as it would have been largely obscured by the rampart. At a height of about 2.3m (7ft 6in) the facing stones are interrupted by a band of five tile courses (*30*). At the top of the wall there was a cornice of tiles – a few fragments of which survive – stepped out one above the other from the wall face. Above the cornice there would again, as at the east corner, have been a parapet. The purpose of the intermediate tile course is a subject of some interest to modern observers, but it is a feature of many Roman walls in Britain and other parts of the empire. The tiles probably fulfilled a structural purpose, binding the core and facing of the wall together. This is why it is only in the walls of the towers on the defences that the tiles go through the full thickness as they are faced on both sides. Although the contrast of buff limestone and red tiles is pleasing to our eyes, the tile courses cannot be decorative and may not even have been visible in Roman times as there is some evidence that the fortress wall, like many stone buildings, was originally rendered or plastered on its outer face.

On the north-west and north-east sides of the defences, associated with the wall described above, the stone towers were about 6m (20ft) square in plan, and set wholly behind the wall, like those of the early second century in the east quadrant. It is likely that there were originally seven towers on the north-west side, but only four have been recorded, the most recently discovered being NW1 in 1971, which is the only one of which remains can be seen today (see p.143 for further comment). The locations of the as yet undiscovered NW4, NW6 and NW7 can be conjectured; presumably the same number of towers existed on the south-east side of the fortress defences, but none has yet been recorded.

On the south-west side of the fortress defences the interval towers represent a much higher level of architectural ambition than those on the other three

37 Interval Tower SW5, looking north-east, as excavated in 1974 (2m scale)

sides. Projecting outwards from the fortress wall line there were great polygonal towers at the west and south corners – the former still visible as the Multangular Tower *(colour plates 3 and 6)* – and six interval towers *(37)*. All but one of these – SW4 – has been seen in recent years, and a few courses of SW6 are visible today in the Museum Gardens. In plan the corner towers had a complex design based on a fourteen-sided figure; a circle through the internal angles would be tangential to the curve of the inner face of the fortress wall. Four of the fourteen faces were omitted at the rear of the towers to create the access to a very substantial structure, rectangular in plan, which lay behind the fortress wall. The projecting parts of the interval towers had a plan designed as half of a twelve-sided figure.

These projecting towers which are found in many other Roman fortifications, usually of the third century and later, are a graphic indication of changing ideas on military strategy. In contrast to earlier times when it fought its enemy in the field, by the end of the second century the Roman army began to expect sieges of its forts and fortresses in a manner which would one day be replicated in medieval warfare. The towers enabled defenders to fire missiles along the line of the walls – to enfilade is the technical term – at any hostile forces attempting to scale or undermine them.

There is sufficient evidence to show that the south-western defences were planned in accordance with metrological principles employed elsewhere in the fortress. It is striking that once again there was a preference for a 35pM (10.36m) unit. As noted in Chapter 2, the distance north-west/south-east across

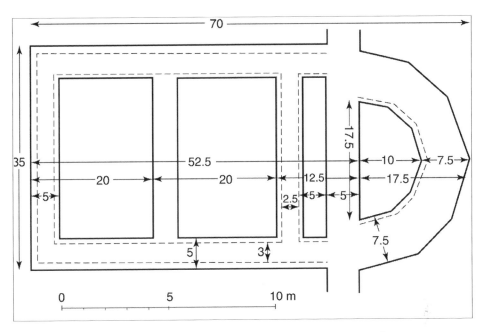

38 Simplified plan of Interval Tower SW5 showing measurements in Roman feet

the fortress prior to construction of a wall was 1,400pM (1,360pM of internal space and 40pM of rampart). When the wall was added this rose to 1,405pM (415.88m) and it appears that for the purposes of spacing the towers on the south-west front this distance was divided into nine units, eight of 160pM (47.36m) and a ninth in the centre of 125pM (37m). The end units were then modified to take the projecting corner towers. The overall length of these corner towers was probably 85pM (25.16m), but they also measured 70pM (2 x 35pM; 20.72m) from the rear of the tower to where a 90° corner to the fortress would have lain. The front of the tower projected 15pM (4.44m) beyond this point. The diameter of the circle joining the internal angles was probably 35pM and the corresponding external diameter at the tower base was 50pM (14.8m).

Each of the six units of wall measuring 160pM contained a stretch of wall 125pM long and an interval tower 35pM wide and 70pM long. The towers projected 17.5pM beyond the wall line which brought them to within 2.5pM (0.74m) of the inner edge of the realigned fortress ditch (see below). The original height of the interval and corner towers is of course not known, but 35pM would answer the requirements of symmetry. However, whether this is an accurate surmise or not, enough is known to show that the size of these corner and interval towers was extraordinary and to prompt the question of why such huge structures were needed. Was this monumental architecture for its own sake or were they intended to fulfil some as yet undetermined military function?

As already noted, although found in several places, the only complete cross-sections of the fortress ditches have been recorded at Interval Towers

SW5 *(39)* and SW6, and they clearly show that a new line was established approximately 5.3m (17ft 6in), measured centre to centre, outside the first (late first-century) ditch. The new ditch was about 6m (19ft 6in) wide and 2.80m (9ft) deep. The reason for moving the ditch outwards is probably to do with ensuring the stability of the wall, but in particular with making space for the projecting towers on the south-west front. As proof of this the ditch appears to have curved outwards slightly around the south and west corner towers. Pottery from the ditch suggested it was silting up, perhaps after a period when it had been kept cleaned out, in the mid-third century. The ditch was then re-cut on the same line.

As far as the rampart is concerned, this has been examined on more occasions than the ditch and it was apparently reconstructed at the same time as the fortress wall. Once the wall had been built in front of the first (late first century) rampart, the space between them was backfilled and the new rampart then built up over both the backfill and first rampart. The new rampart was made wider than the first rampart – about 10-12m (33-39ft) as opposed to 6m (19ft 6in). There also appears to have been some variation in the height of the new rampart. The excavations at St Leonard's Hospital on the south-west side of the fortress in 2003 indicated that the rampart had reached the top of the adjacent fortress wall, the rear face of which was, as noted above, left roughly finished because it was not going to be visible. By contrast, the excavations at the east corner found what appeared to be a cobbled path about 2m (6ft) below the top of the wall along which soldiers patrolling in this area, at least, could circulate without the immediate threat of any missiles from outside reaching them *(34)*. As also noted above, the rear of the wall at the east corner has neat facing stones suggesting it was intended to be visible. In spite of any variations in width or height, however, the new rampart was composed

39 Cross-section through the realigned fortress ditch of the late second – early third century and later re-cuts at Interval Tower SW5 looking south-east (scale 0.50m). The base of the ditch is represented by the slight step to the right of centre. The deepest ditch is the first re-cut, note the typical military profile with an 'ankle-breaker' slot at the base

of layers of material containing a good deal of refuse and so there is plenty of pottery for dating purposes. It tells a consistent story of reconstruction in the late second to early third century.

Claims for a later third- or even early fourth-century date for the wall and towers on the south-west side of the fortress (and other stretches where the construction method was similar) which will be found in some archaeological literature have been, it should be stressed, based on very sparse archaeological evidence: two late third-century coins allegedly found in the rampart but which closer study has shown to be of doubtful origin and a piece of a mortarium (mixing bowl) from the rampart excavated by Miller in the 1920s now re-dated to the late second to early third century. In addition, however, dating has been based on the stylistic affinities of the projecting towers usually thought, in a military context at least, to belong to the later third and fourth century in Britain. Other examples are found at coastal forts such as Cardiff and Portchester Castle. While stylistic arguments cannot be completely dismissed, the dating evidence for York's projecting towers from the associated rampart and ditch is beginning to make an early third-century date look convincing and the great fortress at York may now be seen as leading the way in introducing an important aspect of what was to become common in the late Roman military architecture of Britain.

To conclude, the best interpretation of the dating evidence we have at present is that by the reign of Septimius Severus (193-211) or shortly after, the late first-century earth and timber defences of the fortress at York had been completely refurbished with stone structures. It is just possible that the historical context for completion of the work, including the great projecting towers on the south-west front, was the visit of the emperor himself to York in 208-11. He may have had in mind the need to strengthen York against any possibility of recurring disloyalty by the British legions who had supported Clodius Albinus, his rival for the throne in the year 193, or simply a desire to make his mark on a distant province favoured by his presence. The fact that the towers were confined to the south-west side of the fortress may have reflected the army's opinion that the river was the most likely avenue of attack, but they were probably designed as much to impress local residents – especially those in the town on the opposite bank of the Ouse – and visitors to York with the might and splendour of the empire as to actually deter a siege which could, after all, only be effectively mounted by a Roman army.

THE BARRACKS

In addition to a widening of the rampart, the *intervallum* space itself was widened. This can be most easily explained by saying that in the late first-century fortress the distance between the outer edge of the rampart and the buildings in the fortress was 16.3m (53ft 6in) of which some 6m (20ft 3in) was occupied by the rampart itself and 10.36m (34ft) by the *intervallum*. Following the reconstruction of the defences described above the distance became 22-25m (72ft 1in-82 ft), of which, as noted, about 10m was rampart and 12-15m *intervallum*. This meant that when the timber structures were rebuilt in stone the barracks were reduced in length by about 8% to about 71.25m (233ft) from about 78m (256ft) that they had been in the late first century. The new barracks were, however, wider; a pair of stone barracks at Davygate (including the alley separating it from the next pair) on the south-west side of the fortress was some 31.5m (103ft 4in) wide as opposed to a suggested 25m (82ft) for the earlier timber barracks. This greater width is confirmed by discoveries at 9 Blake Street.

In discussing the late first-century timber structures at 9 Blake Street (p.46) we have already seen that, in addition to the ends of two barrack blocks, there were two ranges, one of which was identified as living quarters and the other as a kitchen. This arrangement appears to have been repeated after reconstruction in stone *(40-2)*. The plan of the stone structures was, moreover,

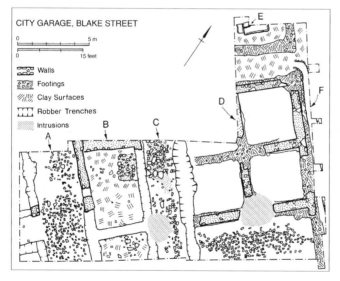

40 9 Blake Street plans:

a) showing the stone buildings found.

A= street
B = kitchen block
C = passage
D = residential block
E = cistern
F = drain

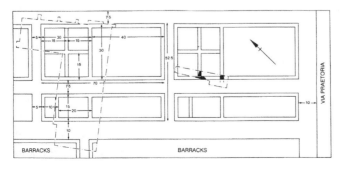

b) a theoretical reconstruction of the intended layout (including an adjacent area to the south-east) with measurements in Roman feet

41 9 Blake Street: stone buildings looking north-west. The main room in the residential block with the opus signinum floors and secondary dividing walls is clearly visible (in the foreground a medieval well dug down from a higher level)

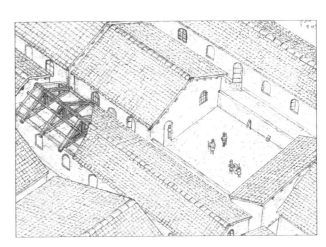

42 9 Blake Street: reconstruction of the fortress buildings (looking north). The ends of the barrack blocks are at the bottom, the narrow kitchen range is shown with the roof partly cut away to show the trusses, and the residential range is in the centre

much better preserved than that of their timber predecessors. By identifying the likely measurements in Roman feet it is possible to suggest the principles on which the former were laid out and reveal, once again, the army's almost obsessive interest in regularity and symmetry *(40b)*.

The corners of two stone barrack blocks were located at the south-west corner of the site and, allowing for a portico 10pM (2.96m) wide along the *via praetoria*, it would have been possible to fit a pair of barracks 105pM (31.08m) wide, or slightly more, into the space north-west of that portico. North-east of the barracks ran the north-west/south-east street, which was 10pM, wide and on its north-east side were the two ranges of buildings. Working from south-west to north-east we find that the overall width of the buildings was probably 52.5pM (1½ x 35pM), the kitchen range being 15pM (4.44m) wide, the alley 7.5pM (2.22m) wide and the main block 30pM (8.88m) wide. A pleasing hier-archy of dimensions is, therefore, apparent; the residential range was twice the width of the kitchen range which was twice the width of the alley between them which was in turn ¾ of the width of the street to the south-west.

If we now work across the 9 Blake Street site from north-west to south-east we find, first of all, that there was the wall of a building which mostly lay beyond the site. This was followed by a narrow alley 5pM (1.48m) wide and then the north-west wall of the building about which we know most. It was 30pM to the next major building line, after which there was possibly a cobbled yard. Going back to the north-west edge of the alley we find that the distance from here to the north-west edge of the presumed portico along the *via praetoria* was 150pM (44.4m). It may be conjectured that the space was divided into two units 75pM (22.2m) long, each designed to be occupied by buildings 70pM (2 x 35pM) long and 52.5pM wide plus an alley 5pM wide on their north-west sides. In this case the favoured 35pM unit crops up again in the diagonal across a building unit 70pM x 52.5pM which is 87.5pM (2½ x 35pM).

Two unusual discoveries were made in the principal room of the stone-built residential range. The first consisted of 35 silver coins found in a restricted area of the footings of the south-west wall. They dated from between 66 BC and AD 79, the latter date being some 70 years or so earlier than the date pottery has given for the construction of the building itself. It is possible that the coins were treasured possessions which had been kept for this period of time before being buried intentionally as an offering for the good fortune of the building. Alternatively they may have been disturbed from an earlier votive hoard and then perhaps reburied for fear of offending the gods. The second unusual dis-covery was a human infant skeleton buried in the floor. The burial of infants in Roman buildings is a well-known phenomenon as it seems they were not con-sidered fully human and so did not have to be buried in the cemeteries outside settled areas. Infant burials are, however, rare in a military context, although not unknown. In this case we may have another form of votive offering to encour-age the gods to look favourably on the residents. It is presumed that the infant died of natural causes and was not a deliberate sacrifice.

At some stage which cannot be closely dated, the principal room in the residential range at the Blake Street site was divided into four smaller rooms, but whether this meant a change of building function is unclear.

SEPTIMIUS SEVERUS IN YORK

Although it is difficult to associate any specific archaeological discovery in York with the visit of the emperor Septimius Severus in 208-11, the events of those years are of great interest, especially as they have been a lasting source of civic pride in more recent times. The same William Hargrove who was quoted in Chapter 1 asserted, for example, that 'it was during this residence of Severus that our city shone in its full splendour', while in 1956 Peter Wenham commented on the emperor's funeral in his *Short Guide to Roman York* with the words: 'In some sense that vivid spectacle marked a turning point in the history of the civilised world and York was its setting.'

Severus's intention in coming to York was to use the fortress as a base for punitive campaigns against the Caledonian tribes in the north of Britain who, it has been suggested, had attacked some of the forts both north of Hadrian's Wall and on the Wall itself in the early years of the third century. If such was the case the Romans would, of course, have regarded retribution as warranted and may even have had some notion of returning the British frontier to the line of the Antonine Wall between the Forth and the Clyde. It is, nonetheless, a little surprising that Severus did not leave the campaign to the governor in Britain, but came himself at a time when he was over 60 years of age and in poor health. Having spent most of his life on campaign, however, Severus may have grown accustomed to the thrill of military success and felt the need to show there was life in the old man yet. It would also seem in keeping with what is known of the emperor's character that he was simply curious to see the remote British province which was about as far from his north African birthplace at *Lepcis Magna* (now in Libya) as it was possible to go without crossing the empire's frontiers. In addition, the contemporary writer Cassius Dio implies that Severus wanted to get his sons away from an idle life in Rome. The emperor probably felt that experience of the rigours of a campaign and the gloss of a military triumph would improve the young men's prospects of succession to the throne after their father's death.

Severus would have travelled to York with a huge retinue of both soldiers and civil servants as the empire's seat of government was wherever the emperor happened to be. Amongst the soldiers there would have been a detachment of the Praetorian Guard and one of their number, Septimius Lupianus, named on a sarcophagus from York, had, according to the inscription, been promoted to legionary centurion and may have received this honour while serving here. It is also known that a number of decrees were issued by Severus in Britain, presumably at York, including one for what might appear the fairly mundane matter of the right of a lady in Rome named Caecilia to recover possession of some slaves or servants. During his stay in York the emperor is said in a fourth-century biography, albeit of uncertain reliability, to have resided in a palace or *domus palatina*. No trace of such a building has ever been found but, while it may be revealed one day, it is perhaps most likely that the legionary commander's house (*praetorium*) was used to accommodate the imperial party. This included Severus's empress Julia Domna, in origin a priest's daughter from Emesa in Syria, and their son Antoninus, usually known as Caracalla. Caracalla had been declared co-emperor in 198, but his younger brother Geta was promoted to the same rank in 209 when he was also in Britain. This led to considerable rivalry between the brothers which must have intensified as Severus's health deteriorated.

Matters came to a head on 2 February 211 when the emperor died in York. His death was not altogether unexpected, it seems, as quite apart from his poor health Severus had allegedly been warned of impending doom by numerous dreams and omens. According to the biography already referred to, the most vivid warning came after a visit to a temple of Bellona (goddess of war) when in error some black rather than the customary white animals had been prepared for sacrifice. On leaving the temple in dismay Severus then found the animals followed him home, thereby confirming his worst fears.

The demise of an emperor was regarded in the Roman world as an event of cosmic significance given his place half way between men and gods, and the funeral, attended by the whole imperial family, would have been correspondingly splendid. According to Cassius Dio:

> ...his body arrayed in military garb was placed upon a pyre, and as a mark of honour the soldiers and his sons ran about it; and as for the soldiers' gifts, those who had things at hand to offer threw them upon it and his sons applied the fire.

Severus was probably cremated somewhere immediately outside the fortress at York, but his ashes were not buried here and we are told that he was taken to Rome in an urn described by Cassius Dio as made of porphyry (a valuable purple stone) and by the biography referred to above as made of gold. Julia Domna, Caracalla and Geta left Britain with precipitate haste to secure the crown with all thoughts of further conquest in the north forgotten.

While on the subject of urns, we may note that a distinctive artefact of the Severan period in York is the so-called 'head pot' *(colour plate 7)*, a vessel made in the shape of a human head. The heads are usually female and, in some cases at least, are thought to represent the empress Julia Domna; male heads may represent Caracalla. Head pots were often used for the burial of cremated remains and in view of the semi-divine status of the imperial family what could be better than consigning one's friend or relative to the hereafter in the care, in a symbolic sense, of one of its members?

It is thought by pottery specialists Jason Monaghan and Vivien Swan that these head pots are made in a style reminiscent of potting traditions in north Africa. Further evidence for the introduction of north African manufacturing styles at about the time of Severus has been identified by Swan in cooking vessels, especially flat casserole dishes with lids. They have an exterior flange at the junction of side wall and base which served to hold them steady while in use on the sort of fired clay brazier used for cooking in the north African provinces. This contrasts with the usual British mode of cooking using a vessel set in hot ashes. Who the potters making these vessels were is not clear, but one possibility is that they belonged to detachments of men sent to join the Sixth Legion at York by Septimius Severus, an emperor who would be certain of the loyalty of men from the part of the empire in which he was born. Swan has also identified vessels, primarily mortaria (mixing bowls), cooking jars and serving bowls, probably made by a potter from the Rhineland, which indicates that the emperor's army also drew reinforcements from this area for its campaigns. The fate of these men stranded in a remote province after their patron had gone to his divine reward is unknown.

CHAPTER 4

THE CIVILIAN SETTLEMENTS

ROMAN SETTLEMENTS AND ROMAN TOWNS: QUESTIONS OF DEFINITION

From the time of its foundation the Roman fortress at York would have exercised a powerful influence on the lives of the local people. On the one hand, the soldiers would have regarded them as a source of manual labour, food and other supplies. On the other hand, many members of the native community would have seen the requirements of the army as an opportunity for personal enrichment and social advancement. It is in this relationship of mutual dependence that we may find the origin of the permanent civilian settlements at York. As time went on the relationship remained close, but it continued to evolve as historical circumstances changed.

In the late first and early second centuries native people occupying land in the York region would presumably have been under strict military control whether actually in a legionary *territorium* (see p.53) or not. In due course, this control was relaxed and the population acquired a considerable degree of autonomy in running their own affairs. In the early second century the Brigantes and Parisi were constituted as self-governing communities with administrative centres at Aldborough (*Isurium Brigantum*) and Brough-on-Humber (*Petuaria*) respectively. The north's largest Roman settlement was, however, to develop at York and by the early third century it was performing a number of distinctive economic, political and social roles in the region arising out of its status as a provincial capital and base of the Sixth Legion. By the end of the fourth century the distinctive character of York's role had been largely eroded by the collapse of the military and political system which supported it; the Roman army had been reorganised in such a way that any soldiers remaining in the fortress were no more than a local militia and there may have been little distinction between the status of people living inside and outside the fortress.

It is customary to refer to the Roman civilian settlements at York as a town and the autonomy referred to in the previous paragraph may be considered a fundamental characteristic of an urban community. It is, however, only one of many and some discussion of how a town may be defined in a Roman context is now required.

Although most people in Britain today live in towns and might feel they know what a town is, it is none the less difficult to give a clear-cut definition of what sets a town apart from other settlements. Factors such as population size, economic and social role, amenities and social organisation must all be taken into consideration and may be given different emphasis according to historical circumstances. As far as the Roman period is concerned, towns have usually been defined, first of all, as places with a distinct legal status which acted as centres of government and administration for their regions. These places were not, however, a homogeneous group, but were incorporated into the Roman social and governmental system by being graded according to the rights and privileges of their inhabitants. This grading was, to some extent at least, reflected in the variety of amenities a place possessed.

At the lowest level of the urban hierarchy were the capitals of the *civitates*, the self-governing communities, such as the Brigantes and Parisi, whose physical boundaries were based on those existing in the pre-Roman period. At the time they were created in the first and early second centuries the vast majority of the inhabitants of the *civitates* were not Roman citizens, but known as *peregrini* (aliens). The next grade up in the hierarchy was the *municipium*, in which the inhabitants might have so-called 'latin rights' giving them a superior legal status to the *peregrini*. Verulamium (St Albans) is thought to have been the only British *municipium*, although the fourth century writer Aurelius Victor described York as a *municipium* at the time of Septimius Severus's visit.

The highest level in the urban hierarchy was the *colonia* (colony). Some part, at least, of the civilian settlement at York had acquired this title by the year 237, the date of an altar dedicated to a local deity, the Tutela Boudiga, at Bordeaux (at the mouth of the river Garonne in south-west France) by Marcus Aurelius Lunaris. He describes himself as a *sevir augustalis*, or priest of the cult of the emperor, at the *coloniae* of both York and Lincoln *(43)*. The likely historical context for York's promotion to *colonia* status was its assumption of the role of capital of *Britannia Inferior* (Lower Britain) in the reign of the emperor Caracalla (211-17) when Britain, originally a single province, was divided into two.

York was henceforth the seat of the Roman governor of *Britannia Inferior*. The first man known by name to have filled the post was Marcus Antonius Gordianus (Gordian) from Cappadocia (in Asia Minor), already fairly elderly in Roman terms at the age of 59. Little trace of Gordian's sojourn can be detected in the city's archaeology, except for a curious inscribed block now built into the foundations of the Minster. It appears to refer to a college of *beneficiarii*, soldiers who were entrusted with special missions, which had named themselves after him. Gordian may well have thought of his position at York as the crowning achievement of his career, but fate was to have another card to play because in 238, some 20 years after his period in York, at the grand old age of 81, he became emperor for a year and even then he died by suicide rather than natural causes!

43 The altar in Yorkshire millstone grit dedicated at Bordeaux in 237 to the Tutela Boudiga by Marcus Aurelius Lunaris, *sevir augustalis* of the *coloniae* at York and Lincoln. Found at Bordeaux in 1921

In origin, the *coloniae* had a distinctive role in the politics and administration of the provinces. Their essential component was a body of Roman citizens willing to promote the interests of the Roman state. In the imperial era a *colonia* was usually created in one of three ways. In the early part most *coloniae* in, for example, the provinces of Gaul and Spain, were settlements of urban character which were promoted on receiving an influx of Roman citizens, usually army veterans or people of Italian origin. In Britain and Germany, which had less sophisticated and more scattered populations at the time of the Roman conquest, *coloniae* were usually created on or adjacent to the sites of Roman military establishments and the bulk of the early colonists was made up of veterans. In Britain there were three first-century *coloniae* (at Colchester, Gloucester and Lincoln) which were built directly on the site of fortresses once their legions had moved on. Finally, in the second and third centuries it became common practice in all provinces of the empire to promote towns of low status to the rank of *colonia*, usually to enable them to fulfil some new political function. York has traditionally, if not necessarily correctly, been thought to fall into this third group. In any event, however, the circumstances of its origins appear to be rather different from those of the other British *coloniae*.

In addition to having a distinct legal status, Roman towns were also centres of population, although in Britain they were never able to compete with the great cities of the Mediterranean littoral or even with the larger towns of

Gaul and the Rhineland. It is unlikely that any town in Roman Britain, even London, ever had more than about 10,000 inhabitants and most probably peaked at about 2-3,000, although such figures represent unusual concentrations of population by the standards of the time.

As noted above, people were probably attracted to urban living by opportunities for enrichment and advancement, and also by the security offered by places under the aegis of the Roman state. It has been argued, however, that in economic terms Romano-British towns were principally centres of consumption rather than production and that a large proportion of their inhabitants were members of the Roman and native land-owning class and their retainers, rather than an urban proletariat. The Romano-British towns were, the argument continues, essentially parasitic, living off local tax revenues and enjoying both the fruits of local agriculture and the lion's share of any luxury goods imported from abroad but giving little back to the people of their hinterlands. The archaeological evidence certainly supports a picture of Romano-British towns as centres for foreign trade, at least as far as the first, second and early third centuries are concerned. There is also evidence from York and elsewhere, however, for towns in this same period as centres for a wide range of crafts and industries which presumably formed the basis of some mutually beneficial economic integration of towns with their regions. At the same time the health of the Romano-British urban economy must have been heavily dependent on construction work for public buildings, residential accommodation and defences, funded either from the public purse or more usually from the private wealth derived from agricultural surplus accruing to the upper echelons of native society. By the mid-third century the support provided by interregional trade and major construction work was no longer at the level it had been hitherto and it may be for this reason that by the mid-fourth century many towns in Roman Britain appear to have been places with a somewhat diminished size and status compared to their first- and second- century forebears.

In spite of their small size relative to those in other provinces, there is no doubt that Romano-British towns had a distinctive appearance which derived from a classical ideal shared with towns throughout the empire. Their most obvious feature was, perhaps, the rectilinear street grid which divided the urban area into *insulae* (islands). The central *insulae* were usually occupied by the major public buildings which included the forum, a building comparable in form to a fort or fortress headquarters where government and the administration of justice took place. It usually existed as a courtyard which served as a market or place of public assembly, surrounded on three sides by rows of shops or offices, the fourth side being occupied by the basilica. In *insulae* adjacent to the forum there would usually be a public bath house, temples and, although rare in a British context, a theatre. *Insulae* surrounding these public buildings would have accommodated domestic residences, shops and workshops.

Romano-British town government was also based on an empire-wide model ultimately derived from Rome itself. There was an *ordo*, nominally of a hundred men known as decurions who were admitted to office on the basis of a property and wealth qualification. From funerary inscriptions we know the names of two decurions from York: Flavius Bellator and Claudius Florentinus, the latter being the son-in-law of the Sixth Legion camp prefect Antonius Gargilianus. Private, as opposed to state funding of public works and festivals by the decurions and other wealthy people was very much the norm in many parts of the Roman empire and towns benefited from the competition between rich men struggling to outdo each other. In Britain, however, private munificence was less common due perhaps to the relative poverty of the native aristocracy or its failure to be impressed by the virtues of urban living. The private funding of construction that is recorded on inscriptions from York and elsewhere was largely devoted to temples.

The characteristics of Romano-British towns outlined above that made them distinct from, as opposed to similar to, their cousins in the Mediterranean heartland of the empire – small size, a fragile economic base and an urban leadership which either lacked funds or Romanised civic values – may be seen, to some extent at least, as products of the artificial nature of their origins. Roman civilisation at the time of the conquest of Britain was based on a governmental system under which the provinces were ruled by town-based elites united by a common culture transmitted by the Greek or Latin languages. These elites were also united in a common social structure based on the privileges of Roman citizenship. In return for these privileges they collected taxes for the state, and rendered military and other public services. The lower orders were kept in check by regular episodes of public generosity which provided food and entertainment – the 'bread and circuses' of the satirist Juvenal's memorable phrase.

In Britain the Romans encountered a country without towns and so, in order to govern and tax it, towns had to be created. At the same time, it was hoped that the leaders of native society could be encouraged to live in towns, to take responsibility for their construction, to assume public office and, in short, become Romans. In the south and east of Britain the progress of town foundation was rapid in the second half of the first century. The sites chosen had usually been occupied by forts or fortresses and were close to, if not on top of, major native settlements. In some cases these settlements, often known as *oppida*, had, as in pre-Roman Gaul, concentrations of population and a variety of functions which brought them close to becoming towns before the conquest.

In the northern and western parts of Britain there were no *oppida*, with the exception of Stanwick (see p.23), and this is probably one reason why urbanisation here was rather slower to take off and was ultimately less successful. The pre-Roman tribal groupings in the north, the Brigantes and the Parisi, had had little experience of living in large settled communities; furthermore they had relatively little experience of the economic activities such as long–distance trade or the use of coinage which, up to a point, characterised *oppida* and Roman towns alike. As already noted, it was not until the early second century that *civitas* capitals were established at Aldborough and Brough-on-Humber. Once founded, moreover, these towns did not catch up with those in the south and east of Britain, and remained small and relatively poorly furnished with civic amenities. York appears to have been very different in character from Aldborough and Brough largely because of its distinct role in provincial and imperial affairs.

THE CIVILIAN SETTLEMENTS AT YORK: NORTH–EAST OF THE OUSE

An account of how the Roman civilian settlements at York developed may begin on the north-east bank of the Ouse. In the previous chapter it was suggested that the legionary fortress was surrounded by a *territorium*, an area of land under direct military control, and that close to the fortress defences a settlement grew up, initially to service the army's needs. In the *Eburacum* volume (see p.18) RCHME described this settlement as the *canabae*, translated as 'booths' or 'stalls'. Whether the Romans ever actually used the word *canabae* to refer to any part of York is, however, unknown, although its use is known in connection with fortresses elsewhere in the empire. None the less, RCHME may not have been too far off the mark in characterising the early settlement around the fortress at York as one which 'housed the motley crowd of tradesmen and purveyors wont to gather about any large military force'.

Although the evidence remains sparse, a picture of the development of Roman settlement north-east of the Ouse is beginning to emerge from archaeological investigations. In Chapter 2 we noted the grain warehouse on the banks of the river, found at 39-41 Coney Street, which belonged to the late first to early second century, and we may imagine that the Ouse was lined with a number of similar structures throughout the Roman period. Evidence for the commercial use of the river Foss is, however, slight and its banks probably remained marginal land until the third century.

Traces of other timber structures, largely in the form of post-holes, of similar date to the Coney Street warehouses are few, being restricted to examples on the corner of Spurriergate and High Ousegate (Site 7 on *1*), south of the south corner of the fortress, and on two sites north-west of the fortress at 31-7 Gillygate and at St Mary's Abbey (Sites 1-2 on *1*). However, the distribution of artefacts, principally pottery, may also be taken into account to plot areas of activity and settlement, and for the early years of the Roman period in York, north-east of the Ouse, these areas appear to have been concentrated close to the south-east, south-west and north-west sides of the fortress and along the lines of the principal Roman approach roads. In addition, located perhaps slightly apart from any settlement were, as we have already seen (p.55), the legionary pottery and tile kilns near the east corner of the fortress.

Growth of the civilian settlement north-east of the Ouse and as we shall see, south-west of the Ouse, appears to have taken off in the late second to early third century. This was apparently marked by some degree of reorganisation of the area south-east and south-west of the fortress. The second phase of the grain warehouse at 39-41 Coney Street was replaced by a gravel street with a fine stone drainage gutter along one side. This street presumably ran along the north-east bank of the Ouse and it was also recorded at the site, referred to above, on the corner of High Ousegate and Spurriergate where it overlay the earlier timber building. This site also revealed a second street which joined the first at an angle of about 90° and probably ran north-eastwards, roughly parallel to the fortress defences. Little is known of buildings around these streets, but parts of substantial stone structures, including a possible bath house, were observed in the High Ousegate/Spurriergate area. Other buildings clearly included temples, including one dedicated to Hercules as is clear from an inscription found in Nessgate (Site 9 on *1*). The names of the two men who sponsored the temple are unfortunately incomplete, but they clearly had some official status, perhaps as members of a college of priests, in a settlement which, although it may have once been under military control, had now become autonomous. Another inscription from Nessgate, entirely appropriate for a temple in a self-governing community, is dedicated to both a goddess, probably local, whose name begins with the letters IOV, and to the spirits of the emperors (*numinibus augustorum*). These emperors could be Marcus Aurelius and Lucius Verus, who ruled jointly from 161-169, but they are perhaps more likely to be Septimius Severus and Caracalla. An altar found a short distance to the north of Nessgate, in Parliament Street, was dedicated by a man named Quintus Creperius Marcus to the *genius loci*. Dr Roger Tomlin has commented that the family name Creperius was common in Africa and Rome itself and so he may have been a soldier from one of these places appealing to the spirit of his new home.

Substantial stone buildings were not necessarily confined to the zone south and south-east of the fortress, as some traces were found in the excavations of the 1950s in the grounds of St Mary's Abbey north-west of the fortress. They included a truly monumental wall some 2m thick interpreted as part of the defences of a fortress annexe (pp.48-9), but more likely to be part of a public building.

In zones apparently peripheral to the main settlement areas outside the fortress there is nonetheless evidence for a markedly higher level of activity than hitherto from the late second century onwards. At 16-22 Coppergate, a site best known for its later, Viking Age remains, ceramic vessels for melting glass were found suggesting glass manufacturing in the vicinity in the early third century. In the mid-third century it appears that what had hitherto been marginal land sloping fairly steeply down to the river Foss and largely used for refuse dumping was divided up with ditches and saw the construction of a stone building with several rooms. Unfortunately, later disturbance had removed all evidence for floor levels so one can only conjecture that this was a residence for a member of what was still an expanding population. Some 230m (250 yards) north-east of Coppergate, at Garden Place, Hungate (Site 8 on *1*), on another site near the Foss, excavations in 1950 located what was probably an artificial channel lined with timber piles in which, perhaps, small boats on the river could have been drawn up. Adjacent to the channel a rectangular stone structure measuring about 7m x 4.57m (23ft x 15ft) with walls of stone blocks 1.5m (5ft) thick has been interpreted as the base for a crane used for lifting cargoes on and off those boats.

Excavations at 21-33 Aldwark (Site 4 on *1*), near the east corner of the fortress, revealed a road laid out on a north-west/south-east line in the late second century, although the site was still otherwise open ground and deemed suitably remote from settlement for a human burial. In the early third century, however, an additional road was laid out on a north-east/south-west line. Contemporary with this was a deposit of pottery waste originating in the nearby kilns (see above) and waste was also found at two other sites nearby on Peasholme Green (No.5 on *1*) suggesting a considerable production episode at about the time of Septimius Severus (see pp.80-1). Also amongst the finds from the Aldwark site was a small group of broken moulds used for making coins of Septimius Severus and Caracalla. Strictly speaking these would have been forgeries, although minting may have been sanctioned locally because of the shortage of supply from the centre.

North-east of the fortress little evidence has yet been found for Roman buildings, but at a large site 2,750 square metres (3,300 square yards) in extent known as County Hospital, Foss Bank (Site 3 on *1*) there was an episode of land division by means of ditches in the late second to early third century. These ditches, typically 0.5m-2m (1ft 6in-6ft 6in) wide and 0.25m-1m (9in-3ft 3in) deep, had largely been dug on the same alignment as the principal axes of the fortress (i.e. north-east/south-west and north-west/south-east). Their purpose may have been partly to drain land prone to flooding and partly to create small land units, perhaps used as fields; a ditch keeps browsing and grazing animals away from crops as well as defining ownership. 'Field ditches' of similar date and alignment have also been found on many other sites adjacent to the main Roman settlement zones at York, north-east and south-west of the Ouse and east of the Foss. They should perhaps be seen as another aspect of the growth of population evident from the late second century onwards in the sense that an increasing demand for food demanded a more intensive use of agricultural land and a shift from pasture to arable. The use of ditches to divide up the landscape does not on the whole, however, seem to have lasted much beyond the mid-third century. Whether this implies some further change in the agricultural regime is unclear.

THE CIVILIAN SETTLEMENTS AT YORK: SOUTH–WEST OF THE OUSE — ORIGINS

For the sake of convenience the civilian settlement on the south-west bank of the Ouse is usually referred to as the *colonia*, although in origin it presumably had some other legal title. Strictly speaking, moreover, the extent of the Roman settlement that *colonia* status encompassed is unknown, although the area enclosed by the medieval walls south-west of the Ouse has usually been designated as the *colonia* to the exclusion of all others (for a plan showing Roman sites within the medieval walls south-west of the Ouse see *40*). This designation has arisen principally because the inscribed coffin of Flavius Bellator, described as a *decurion* of the *colonia*, was recovered from the Roman cemetery adjacent to the city walls on the site of the present railway station. It must be considered a distinct possibility, however, that the civilian settlement on the north-east bank of the Ouse, described above, also received *colonia* status at or about the same time as that on the south-west bank. If inscribed stone coffins are to be used as evidence, then some support for this proposal may be supplied by the stone coffin of another decurion (whose name is incomplete) discovered re-used in a medieval cemetery at a site on Fishergate, north-east of the Ouse (and also east of the Foss), but perhaps brought from the Roman cemetery nearby.

On the south-west bank of the Ouse it is likely that the surviving medieval defences define what became at least part of the *colonia* since, for the most part, they probably correspond to and overlie a Roman defensive circuit. York is unusual amongst medieval towns in England in having walls sited on top of a pre-existing rampart rather than at ground level. An excavation on the city and Roman fortress defences (north-east of the Ouse) near the Anglian Tower (see pp.142-3) has shown that this is because of the existence of the fortress wall below later Viking Age and Norman ramparts. By analogy it is likely that a similar sequence exists south-west of the Ouse with a *colonia* wall as the earliest feature. It must be admitted, however, that a Roman wall has only been seen in three places beneath the later rampart, all of which were on the north-west side of the enclosure and in no case in the context of a properly controlled excavation.

Defences require gates and, although the line of the main approach road from the south-west remains uncertain (p.50), it may be suggested that any main gate to the *colonia* was on or close to the site of medieval Micklegate Bar, which does contain a good deal of re-used Roman stonework. Gates, or at least their sites, are the only feature of Britain's Roman towns, apart from the defensive walls themselves, which regularly survived into the post-Roman period and we already know that all of the fortress gates remained in use, giving the medieval and modern city north-east of the Ouse its distinctive form. There is, unfortunately, no exact dating for these proposed Roman defences south-west of the Ouse, but it is possible that construction took place at the time of the general move to defend the towns of Roman Britain in the late second century. Alternatively, the occasion may have been the granting of *colonia* status, an event which was perhaps thought to demand the display of architectural splendour which defences provided.

The importance for the study of Roman York of the area enclosed by the medieval walls south-west of the Ouse became apparent long before it was identified as a part of a *colonia*. Ever since the Bishophill altar was found in 1638 there have been frequent discoveries of structures and artefacts during building work, although the only systematic archaeological excavation before World War Two was a hurried affair (still unpublished) in 1939 during construction of an Air Raid Control Centre near the Old Station which revealed part of a bath house. The next dig took place in 1962 when Peter Wenham excavated the first of a series of small trenches in the Bishophill district. Another excavation was undertaken by Herman Ramm at St Mary Bishophill Senior (following the demolition of the church) in 1964 and one of the York Archaeological Trust's early excavations also took place in Bishophill. While the main Roman road from the south-west was recorded at 27 Tanner Row in 1970, it was not until 1981 that the first thorough investigation of a site in the heart of the Roman town took place at 5 Rougier Street. Since that year further excavations have confirmed the existence of a well-preserved Roman townscape in this area, and at last the mystery surrounding the history and layout of one of Britain's more important Roman towns has begun to find a measure of resolution.

In spite of recent investigations the origins of Roman settlement south-west of the Ouse remain obscure, although it is possible that in the late first and early second centuries much of the area facing the fortress was deliberately kept clear of buildings for military reasons. Traces of timber structures associated with late first-century pottery were, however, found on the site of the Air Raid Control Centre. The site lay north-west of the main Roman approach road from the south-west and, on purely topographical grounds, this area may be considered as a likely focus of early settlement. Not only was it close to the road, but it was also on high ground commanding a view of the fortress and of the Ouse. In addition the area produced the two small bronze plaques apparently dedicated in the late first century by Scribonius Demetrius (see above p.40), which were probably displayed in a temple or shrine associated with an official building ('the governor's residence' referred to on one of the plaques).

Any zone of late first- or early second-century settlement on the north-west side of the later *colonia* enclosure was probably fairly restricted, although it may have extended along the line of the approach road from the south-west as far as what is now Blossom Street. Observations in 1994 during redevelopment of the site on the north-west side of the street referred to above (Site 13 on *1* and see p.50) revealed a long sequence of Roman remains beginning with the Roman road itself and a street at right angles to it along with remains of buildings which probably belonged to the early second century. On the oppo-

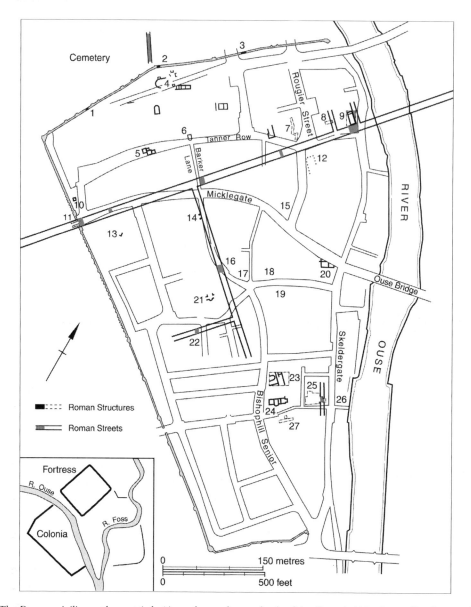

44 The Roman civilian settlement (*colonia*) on the south-west bank of the Ouse (within the medieval city walls) showing the location of archaeological discoveries, principal excavations and streets (known and conjectured).

1 Old Station: defences
2 Air Raid Control Centre: defences
3 Find spot of Mithraic relief of Arimanius and defences
4 Old Station Air Raid Control Centre: baths
5 Toft Green: house with mosaics
6 Temple of Serapis
7 General Accident, Tanner Row: buildings

8 5 Rougier Street: warehouses and street
9 Wellington Row: main road, street and buildings
10 Bar Lane: house with mosaic
11 Micklegate Bar: street
12 George Hudson Street: column bases
13 Kenning's Garage: building
14 Trinity Lane: column bases

15 Micklegate/George Hudson Street: Mithraic relief and column bases
16 Trinity Lane: street
17 St Martin's Lane/Trinity Lane: buildings
18 Fetter Lane: baths
19 Fetter Lane: building
20 1-9 Micklegate: baths
21 St Mary Bishophill Junior: house

22 Bishophill Junior: street and building
23 37 Bishophill Senior: houses and terrace
24 St Mary Bishophill Senior: house
25 58-9 Skeldergate: street and well
26 23-8 Skeldergate: waterfront
27 Friends Burial Ground: structures

45 (left) Wellington Row: a limestone layer, dated to the mid-second century, possibly forming a surface of the main Roman road from the south-west. The view is to the north-west and the road runs from side to side; at the bottom are stone blocks covering the trench for a water pipe (1m scale). *46 (right)* Wellington Row: the lead water pipe in its stone-lined trench, looking north-east (0.50m scale)

site side of Blossom Street another excavation (at Nos 35-41; Site 14 on *1*) produced ditched enclosures and refuse deposits of the first half of the second century. As yet the only possible evidence for an early Roman building south-east of the main approach road comes from a site on Fetter Lane where part of a bath house found in 1852 had a room with a floor of Ninth Legion tiles (Site 18 on *44*).

Just as it was on the north-east bank of the Ouse, the third quarter of the second century was marked by the beginning of a rapid growth of settlement on the south-west bank, taking in areas close to the river for the first time. This has, perhaps, been most dramatically revealed by excavations at Wellington Row, where we may take up once more the history of the main road from the south-west (see p.50). Following the early series of gravel surfaces, a layer of crushed magnesian limestone was laid down and given a hard smooth surface with a camber on its north-west side *(45)*. It is not clear, however, whether this was a road surface as such and it may rather have been intended as a base for further gravel layers. Contemporary with the limestone layer, on the south-east side there was a line of large limestone blocks which served as capping for a trench lined with further blocks. It contained a lead pipe of the type used by the Romans for mains water supply *(46)*. The pipe has an inner diameter of 150mm, one of the largest recorded from Britain. Above the limestone the level was raised by up to 2m (6ft 6in) with layers of cobbles and gravel creating a causeway standing proud of the contemporary ground surface. This must surely have been done to allow the construction, or reconstruction, of a bridge across the Ouse. Raising the level on the south-west bank was necessary because of the significantly higher natural level on the north-east bank (p.26). No certain trace of the bridge itself has been found, although substantial stone structures of uncertain date recorded under York's Guildhall in 1893 may be part of the north-easternmost pier. The discoveries at Wellington Row are of great importance because the establishment of a water supply and construction of a bridge (if this presumption is accurate) represented major investments in infrastructure which may have marked a very significant episode in the history of the settlement, even, it may be suggested, a deliberate urban foundation.

YORK – A LATE SECOND–CENTURY BOOM TOWN

Once the process of settlement had taken off in about the years 150-160, growth over the next 50-60 years was continuous. The evidence does not, however, support the gradual realisation of a single unitary urban plan. Instead it seems likely that there was a series of episodes of expansion, on occasions involving reorganisation of areas already developed, each of which involved the laying out of streets, the construction of buildings and the carrying out of other public works such as drainage and terracing. To illustrate an early episode in the sequence, we may remain on the Wellington Row site and look at discoveries made in 1988-9 in the largest single area ever excavated archaeologically on the south-west bank of the Ouse *(47)*.

One of the earliest features uncovered was a ditch at the north-west end of the site, running towards the river, which may have served both for drainage and as a boundary in some early land division exercise. Another ditch was found running alongside the main road. These ditches were probably roughly contemporary with a small gravel street running north-west/south-east at 90° to the main road. The life of this layout was brief; the ditches filled up with silt and refuse, and the street was moved a few metres to the north-east to accommodate a stone building. Because its walls, standing in places over 2m (6ft 6in) high, and internal floor levels had not, as is usual in York, been heavily disturbed by medieval pits, it was possible to trace the building's long and chequered history in some detail.

As originally constructed, the Wellington Row building measured about 15.5m x 10.5m (51ft x 34ft) and lay end-on to the main road from the south-west *(48)*. It overlay the earlier roadside ditch, and its south-east wall was founded on the edge of the limestone road layer noted above, and the two

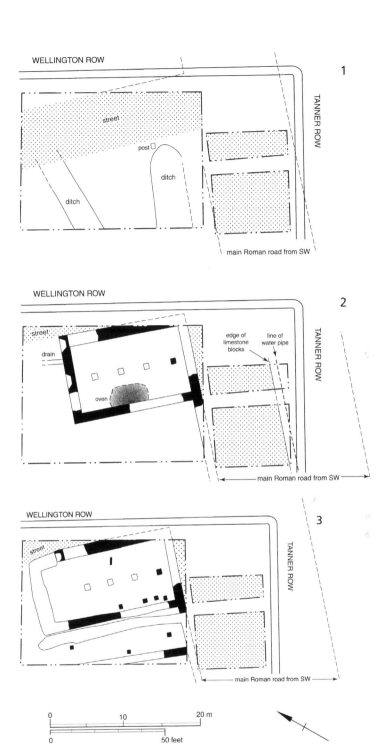

47 Wellington Row plan of development:

1 Mid-second century – ditches and early street
2 Mid to late second century – stone building
3 Late second to early third century – reconstruction of stone building and addition of other structures to the south-west

48 Wellington Row: mid-second-century stone building looking north-west showing (lower left) the location of joists for the timber floor. An oven was located top left and the original north-west wall is obscured by the shoring brace (2m scale)

were probably contemporary. The walls were, in contrast to the road surface, built throughout of oolitic rather than magnesian limestone and were founded on footings of clay and cobble strengthened with timber piles. The main door of the building was probably on its north-east side. Equidistant from the side walls at the south-east end of the building was a substantial pillar composed of three millstone grit blocks. This must have been the base for a roof support, and three other similar pillars had clearly been removed in medieval times as their foundation pits survived. The roof itself was probably composed of sandstone slabs, which were found in abundance. As far as the floor was concerned, the south-eastern third of the building, possibly divided from the rest by a partition, had a timber floor of joists with planks over them. Against the south-west wall was an oven made of clay, presumably for cooking or baking.

The oven was, perhaps, the source of a fire which swept through the building early in its life. Evidence of a fire of a similar late second-century date was also found at 5 Rougier Street, and it is possible that the whole of the immediate area was affected, although sporadic fires were probably a constant hazard in York as in other towns throughout the Roman period. At all events, damage to the Wellington Row building was considerable and, although the debris had been largely cleared away, some charred floor timbers and joists remained. Most striking of all, the walls had gone a pink or, in places, a bright red colour due to the heat.

After the fire the opportunity was taken in the reconstruction process to extend the building 2m (6ft 6in) to the north-west. The upstanding wall of this extension did not survive at all, but a structure of some substance was implied by the construction trench, which was 1.5m (5ft) deep and packed with clay and cobbles. Driven into the base were some 200 timber piles, about 3m (10ft) long, which were mostly oak logs but included some re-used timbers.

1 Column from the north-eastern arcade in the headquarters basilica of the Roman fortress, found collapsed in the Minster excavations (see Illustration *6*) and re-erected outside the Minster south door

2 Modern bronze statue of Constantine, acclaimed Emperor in York in 306, outside the south door of the Minster

3 The Multangular Tower: in origin a
Roman tower at the west corner of the
legionary fortress. The small facing stones
in the lower half are Roman and the
larger stones in the upper half represent
reconstruction in the medieval period

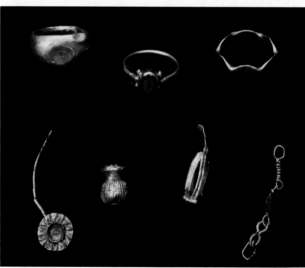

4 Roman gold jewellery from York.
Top row: rings; bottom row: ear-ring,
pendant fitting, ear-ring and pendant
chain (middle two from the Church
Street sewer)

5 Fragments of second-century pottery
vessels in Ebor ware

6 The Multangular Tower interior; the peacock sits on the top of the Roman walling. A fragment of a central spine wall which originally divided the tower into two can be seen. The Roman stone coffins have been collected from a number of Roman cemeteries around York

7 Early third-century head pot, probably representing the empress Julia Domna, wife of Septimius Severus (height 300mm)

8 Conjectural reconstruction of Roman York in the early third century looking north-east. The river Ouse runs across the centre, the fortress is at the top and the civilian settlement (*colonia*) south-west of the Ouse is at the bottom (for further discussion see p.129-30)

9 Reconstruction of the Roman cemetery
on the main approach road to York from the
south-west (where The Mount meets Albemarle
Road today) with the town (*colonia*), shown
walled, in the distance

10 The tombstone of Julia Velva. Found on
The Mount at the junction with Albemarle
Road in 1922 (height 1.68m)

11 *(left)* A head in Magnesian
Limestone thought to be
Constantine I ('the Great'),
proclaimed Emperor in York in
306 (height 0.45m)

12 *(below)* Detail of the Four
Seasons mosaic from Toft Green,
showing Spring

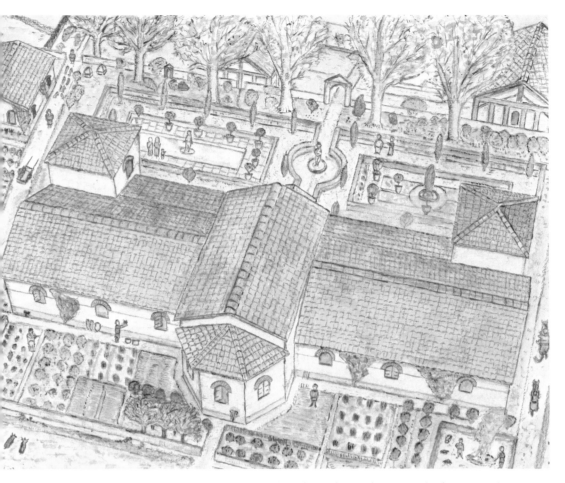

13 Reconstruction illustration of the house excavated at Clementhorpe, showing in the foreground the polygonal apse added to it in the early fourth century. The towers are based on evidence from a similar building at Beadlam villa

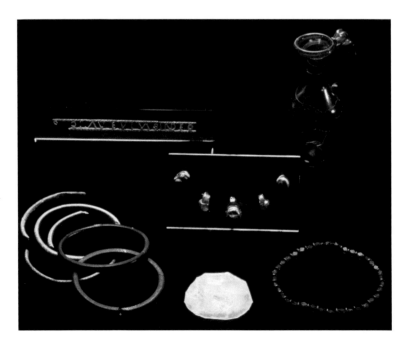

14 A fourth-century grave group (Sycamore Terrace, York) including a small bone plaque with an open work inscription, SOROR AVE VIVAS IN DEO, thought to be Christian in sentiment. In addition there are two jet bangles, a bracelet of blue glass, glass beads, silver and bronze lockets, two yellow glass earrings and a small round crystal mirror

15 Restored painted wall plaster panel from a room added to the north-west side of the basilica of the fortress headquarters (*principia*) in the fourth century, now on display in the York Minster Undercroft near where the fragments were found

16 Fragments of pottery in Crambeck Parchment ware – late fourth-century – showing a human figure, possibly a soldier or a god, depicted in red paint (height 83mm)

It may be conjectured that a grand, even monumental entrance to the building was constructed at its north-west end. At the same time the floor in the build-ing was levelled up with a thick layer of limestone rubble and mortar *(49)*. Set on its surface along the south-west wall were four (originally six) stone blocks, and another longer block was found near the north-east wall. The function of these blocks is unknown; they may, along with others later removed, have supported a suspended timber floor.

When reconstruction of the building took place, several small pits were dug into the rubble and mortar floor, in three cases for the burial of pots and in a fourth for a glass bowl. One of the pots had been buried in a wooden box and was found filled with crushed fish bones, possibly the remains of the fish sauce (*garum*) much loved by the Romans. The burial of vessels is not uncommon in Roman buildings, and they presumably represented further examples of cult practice of the sort already noted at 9 Blake Street in the fortress (p.78), in which offerings were made to the *genius loci* for the good fortune of a building and its occupants.

During the excavation at Wellington Row it was hoped that some distinc-tive finds would identify the function of this building about which so much else was known, but all that is reasonably certain is that it is unlikely to have been either a dwelling or a workshop. One possibility is that it was the meet-ing place for members of a *collegium* or guild who shared a common occupa-tion, perhaps as merchants plying their trade on the Ouse; in other words the building may have been a Roman version of the city's medieval guildhalls.

Further evidence for rapid development of the settlement in the mid- to late second century was revealed in the 5 Rougier Street trench *(50)*. The earliest feature, located at a depth of about 6m (20ft) below modern ground level, was a continuation of the ditch found at Wellington Row which had run alongside the main road from the south-west. In its final phase of use the ditch was given a timber lining. On the south-east side of the trench there were two stone pil-

49 Wellington Row: the stone building as recon-structed after a fire, with a limestone and mortar surface and stone blocks along the walls. The sur-viving roof support pillar is at the south-east end of the building to the right of the picture (2m scale)

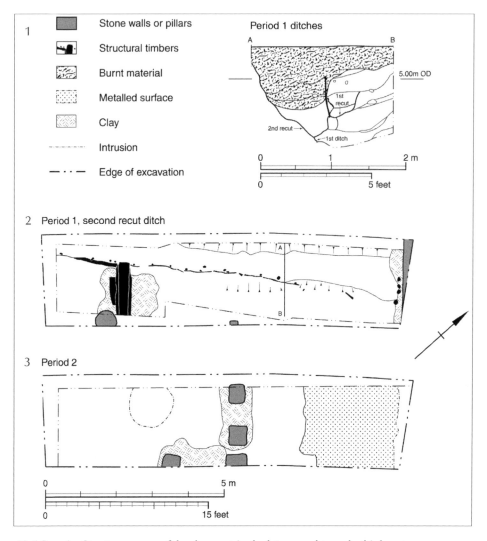

1

■ Stone walls or pillars

Structural timbers

Burnt material

Metalled surface

Clay

------- Intrusion

— · · — Edge of excavation

Period 1 ditches

A   B

5.00m OD

1st recut

2nd recut

1st ditch

0   1   2 m

0   5 feet

2   Period 1, second recut ditch

A

B

3   Period 2

0   5 m

0   15 feet

50 5 Rougier Street: sequence of development in the late second to early third century.

1 Cross-section of mid to late second-century ditch
2 Timber-lined ditch fed by a chute
3 Street running north-west/south-east and stone pillars

lars, in one case made of re-used column drums. They had, perhaps, supported the raised floor of a building standing above the ditch which then served as a drain, being connected to the building by a timber-lined chute. It was common practice in Roman times to raise the floors of warehouses off the ground both to keep vermin out, and, by allowing the air to circulate, prevent a build-up of dampness. The ditch finally went out of use when it was cut across by a very substantial wall, with a base course of massive millstone grit blocks, running north-west/south-east at the north-east end of the trench. Both the wall and pillars were succeeded by a thick dump of burnt material composed largely of

51 5 Rougier Street looking north-east: stone pillars which probably supported a warehouse floor facing the street, which ran left to right beyond the 1m scale

52 5 Rougier Street: incomplete relief of a cockerel, probably symbolising Mercury, whose feet are just visible, on a small block of magnesian limestone (height 60mm)

grain (see p.104), but also including charred timber. This material probably resulted from the collapse of the warehouse during a fire.

As at Wellington Row there was reconstruction after the fire and this evidently involved an element of replanning in the immediate neighbourhood. The gritstone wall was replaced by a gravel street running north-west/south-east at 90° to the main road. South-west of the street a new warehouse was apparently constructed with a floor again raised on stone pillars *(51)*. If this interpretation of the remains is correct, this building and its predecessor would imply that York was a centre for the collection and marketing of agricultural products in the late second and early third centuries, as is also shown by the evidence from the nearby General Accident site described below. Of some interest in this commercial context was the discovery in the burnt deposit of part of a small stone relief depicting a cockerel bearing little bags on its back *(52)*.

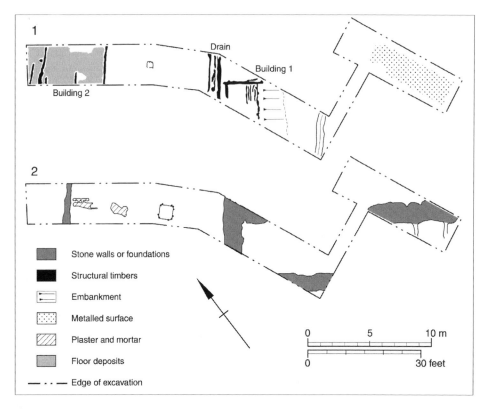

1

Drain

Building 1

Building 2

2

Stone walls or foundations

Structural timbers

Embankment

Metalled surface

Plaster and mortar

Floor deposits

Edge of excavation

0   5   10 m

0   30 feet

53 General Accident, Tanner Row: plans showing sequence of development in the late second to early third century
1 Late second-century timber buildings, ditch (centre right) and cobbled surface (right)
2 Early third-century stone building.

Above the bird is a pair of feet, which probably belonged to a representation of Mercury. He is frequently accompanied by a cockerel in Roman art and one of his functions was to protect merchants. Mercury was also the messenger of the gods and the messages themselves may have been symbolically contained in the cockerel's bags.

Particularly good evidence for commercial activities and the crafts practised in late second century York came from another excavation very close to the main Roman approach road from the south-west. This was excavated in 1983 in advance of an extension to what was then the General Accident building in Tanner Row (the site is known as 'General Accident' for short). The earliest archaeological feature here was a continuation of the roadside ditch found at Wellington Row and 5 Rougier Street. At the south-east end of the site, beyond the ditch, there was a spread of cobbles probably representing a yard alongside the main road. It appears that horses or cattle were corralled or stabled close by, as the overlying layer consisted largely of hay-rich dung identified on the basis of surviving fibrous matter and insects known to live in stables.

54 General Accident, Tanner Row: late second-century timber buildings (1m scale). The north-east end wall of Building 1 runs diagonally from lower left towards the centre of the picture where it meets a timber-lined drain

55 General Accident, Tanner Row: detail of a post and plank wall of Building 1 (0.50m scale)

Roughly contemporary with the use of the ditch, probably in the 160s, there was an episode of ground preparation which involved raising the level in the centre of the site with layers of turf and clay. This compensated for the gentle natural slope rising from the south-east to north-west and created two level platforms suitable for building, divided by a low timber revetment. Parts of two timber structures were found, although it was not possible to get complete plans of them because of the narrowness of the trenches *(53-4)*. Little upstanding wall survived, as demolition later in the Roman period had been thorough, but it was clear that Building 1, nearest the main road, had been constructed with walls based on sill beams held in position by posts. These posts had also projected upwards and had horizontal planks nailed to them. There was probably a timber plank floor. Immediately to the north-west there was a large timber-lined drain which had been used for the disposal of kitchen waste and human faeces, the presence of the latter being betrayed by large quantities of the eggs of parasitic worms which live in the gut.

To the north-west of the drain Building 2 was found. Its remains were fewer but the bases of two walls survived as timber sill beams resting on layers of clay and stones. At some stage in the late second century Buildings 1 and 2 were reconstructed and one wall in Building 1 was given a form of cavity wall with planks nailed on to both sides of the upright posts *(55)*. The well-preserved timbers in the buildings described here exhibit a wealth of evidence for the techniques of the Roman carpenter; axe and saw marks are common, and there are joints and mortices. However, the timbers had clearly been re-used from elsewhere and one distinct possibility is that some at least come from fortress buildings which were probably being rebuilt in stone at much the same time (p.76).

In the layers around the General Accident buildings there was abundant evidence for craft activity, especially metalworking. Slag from iron smithing and copper working occurred in some quantity along with numerous pieces of metal scrap and iron tools. Leatherworking is attested by large quantities of offcuts and shoe fragments *(56)*. In addition, the complete leather panel of an army tent and scraps of others were found. On one of these scraps careful cleaning by conservators has revealed a graffito scratched into the leather which refers to the Century of Sollius Julianus. This man has been identified as Marcus Sollius Julianus, a centurion named on a building stone on Hadrian's Wall which commemorates a stretch of the Wall built by his men. We have, therefore, a remarkable and unusual testimony to the connection between the Sixth Legion on the Wall and its base in York. Other military equipment from around the General Accident buildings included a pattern-welded iron sword, possibly brought to the site for repair or recycling, and several fittings from military uniforms. In short the evidence is that in the latter part of the second century this part of York was occupied by people engaged in a variety of crafts and a major source of their income may have come from providing manufacturing and repair services to the army.

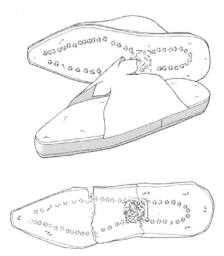

56 General Accident, Tanner Row: drawing of a sole of a sandal with a maker's mark stamped on it. At the top is a reconstruction of the sandal

ROMAN DIET

In addition to material representing crafts, the late second-century layers at General Accident also produced large quantities of food remains, which give an insight into the diet of the period and also into aspects of Roman York's trading contacts. As far as meat is concerned, research by Terry O'Connor of York University into the animal bones from the site has shown that the principal source was beef, supplemented by a little mutton and pork. The proportion of bones (7,306 in total) for the three main meat-providing species collected in late second- to mid-third-century layers is shown in *57*. Other meat was provided by domestic fowl and geese, but there was hardly any evidence for wild animals; only very small numbers of bones from deer, hare and wild birds were found.

In addition to identifying bones to species, O'Connor has also shown that their character can reveal something of the nature of the meat products produced by local butchers, probably on a commercial scale. First of all, there were numerous smashed-up cattle limb bones, the residue of systematic extraction of the marrow, used, perhaps, for some cheap but nourishing food. Secondly, there were large numbers of cattle shoulder blades interpreted as debris from the smoking of shoulders of beef. They are often pierced, showing that the shoulders were hung up for a period, perhaps during the smoking process. O'Connor has suggested this smoked meat was something of a luxury given the expense consequent on the time and labour involved in its preparation.

Based on the size of the bones themselves, O'Connor has suggested that there were two breeds of cattle. One was the so-called 'Celtic Shorthorn' with small, tightly curved horns, a native breed of pre-Roman Britain *(58)*. The other breed was rather more robust with heavier horns and it may have been introduced to Britain in the Roman period. In both cases, however, the beasts were relatively small compared to their modern counterparts with a withers height on average of 1.1m (3ft 6in). This is fairly typical of cattle

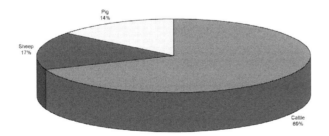

57 Percentage of bones from principal meat providers: mid-second- to early third-century layers, General Accident, Tanner Row (total sample 7,306). *T.P. O'Connor, 1988,* Bones from the General Accident Site, The Archaeology of York 15/2

58 General Accident, Tanner Row: part of the skull of a cow of the 'Celtic Shorthorn' type (max. width 290mm)

before selective breeding began in earnest in the eighteenth century. Breeding has not only made beasts larger, but also given them specialised uses as providers of meat or milk. Roman cattle were essentially multi-purpose, being not only a source of meat, but also milk-producers and beasts of burden. This may explain the relative absence of the bones of young animals under three years old. Cattle were only slaughtered when of no further use alive. Once they were dead, all parts would have been used in some way; hides, for example, went to make leather, and one can envisage a close relationship between the butchers, tanners and shoemakers in Roman York.

Staples of the Roman diet were bread and other dishes with a cereal content. It is appropriate, therefore, that Roman York has produced large quantities of charred cereal grain, two deposits being of particular importance. One was found in the 39-41 Coney Street warehouse (p.54) and consisted, firstly, of about 60% spelt wheat (Latin, *Triticum spelta*). This was the principal Roman cereal grown in southern and eastern Britain and can be distinguished from so-called 'bread wheat', also known in the period, by having grains which are not as easily removed from the ears in harvesting. In addition, about 25% of the Coney Street deposit was barley and about 25% rye. The grain from the ditch at 5 Rougier Street (p.99) consisted of around 89% spelt wheat and about 11% barley. The latter was probably used for brewing, and one can envisage that beer, the traditional British beverage, was as popular as imported wine with the local population. Both grain deposits contained copious seeds of a number of field weeds, including the corncockle. This has a fine pink flower and was common in British fields before the regular use of selective weed killers. The seeds are, however, poisonous and if incorporated in cereal-based foods would have caused a serious Roman stomach ache!

The other weed seeds are interesting, as they show that by the late second century York was having a considerable impact on its surrounding region, drawing its food supplies from a variety of ecological zones, some of which were 25km (15½ miles) and more distant. Seeds of plants which grow on salt marshes probably came from the dung of cattle grazed on meadows near the mouth of the Humber. Seeds which suggest a limestone or chalk land environment may again have come to York in dung from animals driven into the town for slaughter or in the hay brought in to feed the horses, mules and donkeys employed by soldiers and civilians alike. In addition, layers excavated at General Accident and other sites produce seeds from plants suitable for human consumption including opium poppy, coriander, dill and summer savory, all used as food seasoning.

Not all the food eaten in Roman York was locally produced. The General Accident site produced evidence for imports from further afield including crabs, perhaps from Bridlington Bay on the Yorkshire coast, and herring, which were probably caught in the Humber estuary (the bones of deep-sea fish like cod are absent from Roman layers). From beyond Britain, represented by their stones, pips and seeds, came olives, grapes, and figs. Wine does not, of course, survive but numerous sherds of wine amphorae, largely of Gallic origin, are commonly found on sites in the civilian settlements. Compared to our wine today it was probably rather bitter and had to be sweetened and watered down to become palatable. Finally, amongst the bones from the General Accident site there were those of a species of dormouse (Latin, *Eliomys quercinus*) native to Gaul which, while not the classic edible type (Latin, *Glis glis*) mentioned in Roman literary sources, may have been an acceptable substitute (*62*).

Although small in quantity relative to what was locally produced, the evidence for imported food is important as it suggests the presence of a community in which there were people who not only had sophisticated tastes, but also the wealth to gratify them. In this sense the food remains alone indicate that by the end of the second century the Roman civilian settlement at York had acquired a distinct character and status which set it apart from the surrounding rural areas.

TRADING CONTACTS

Many other goods besides foodstuffs would have been traded in Roman York, but in the majority of cases they would have been made of perishable materials which have not survived in the ground. Exceptions amongst the imports include building materials, especially stone (discussed on pp.53-4 above) and pottery, a commodity which survives well and can give some indication of the direction, if not necessarily the volume, of local, interregional and overseas trade. As far as wares of continental origin are concerned, imports in the second to early third century were dominated by samian ware from sources in Gaul (noted on pp.55-6), which was also the source of unusual green glazed

59 Wellington Row: fragments of a second- to third-century green-glazed double handled cup with satyrs in relief (height 100mm)

60 Jet objects from Roman York. The medallions depict (from left to right) a betrothed couple (height 63mm), a gorgon mask and a family group

vessels *(59)*. In addition, the Rhineland, principally Cologne, was the source of what are usually known as colour-coated beakers and jars which have a low relief decoration and a shiny purple finish. At Wellington Row, which produced the largest assemblage of Roman pottery from any single site in York (approximately 20,000 sherds), about 25% from layers of the mid-second to early third century was produced outside Britain and in layers of the mid-third century the figure rises to about 36%. These figures appear to be fairly typical of sites south-west of the Ouse.

Britain was well known to the Romans as a source of grain, and exports from York were probably made up for the most part of agricultural products. There is, however, a more exotic export which was a local speciality. Jet, a mineral akin to coal, was found on the north-east coast of Yorkshire in the Whitby area *(60)*. It can be easily cut and given a high polish. In addition, static electricity is generated when a piece of jet is rubbed, which probably gave it an aura of magic in antiquity. Jet does occur in other parts of Europe, but much of the Roman jet found in the western empire probably came from Britain. While it may have been shipped raw, it is also likely that there were jet workshops in York which exported finished pieces. Among the commoner items were beads, bracelets, hair pins and rings, but more elaborate pieces included medallion pendants bearing human portraits and, most striking of all, gorgon masks which served to repel the evil eye.

To conclude, the archaeological evidence suggests that York's trading contacts, especially over long distances, were at their most extensive in the late second and early third centuries when the economic and political conditions in the western empire still favoured the activities of sea-going merchants. We know the names of a small number of these men from inscriptions. They include Lucius Viducius Placidus, referred to as *negotiator* (merchant) on an inscribed tablet dated to 221 found in excavations at Clementhorpe (Site 15 on *1*), a little to the south-east of the city walls *(61)*. This tablet bears a rare British example of the commemoration of building work by a private individual, in this case an arch and covered passageway (ARCVM ET IANVM) which may perhaps have been a secular urban landmark or part of a temple. The inscription also tells us that Placidus came from the territory of the Veliocasses centred on what is now Rouen in northern Gaul. It is likely that our man gained his citizenship during the reign of the emperor Caracalla, as he is known without the *tria nomina* simply as Placidus, son of Viducus, on an inscription dredged from the Rhine estuary in the Netherlands. In typical native fashion he Romanised his father's name to form the family name (*nomen gentilicium*) Viducius, and Placidus was kept as his familiar name (*cognomen*). One may speculate that his success in the world was based largely on trade across the North Sea involving perhaps the carriage of wine and pottery from Cologne or Trier (now in Germany) to York and return trips with grain, beef and jet jewellery.

61 Stone tablet dated 221 commemorating the construction of an arch and covered passageway by the merchant – (N) EGOTIATOR – Lucius Viducius Placidus from the territory of the Veliocasses (centred on Rouen, northern France). Found at Clementhorpe in 1976 (width 0.63mm)

THE ECOLOGY OF ROMAN YORK

In addition to providing evidence for the consumption and marketing of food-stuffs, the organic matter preserved on the General Accident site is of interest for illustrating the ecological history of the *colonia*. It is clear that over a period of about 50 years there was a radical change from an environment subject to little human influence, beyond perhaps the grazing of stock, to one bearing the imprint of permanent settlement. The most striking witness to this was the increasing occurrence in the superimposed layers on the site of decomposing organic matter which became abundant around the buildings. It probably derived from a number of sources including food remains, human and animal faeces, and the litter from floor-covering and bedding. There was also cereal debris and hay, which must have come from the stabling of horses.

The somewhat squalid environs of the buildings provided ideal habitats for a diverse fauna which enjoyed the company of humanity. An enormous variety of insects included house flies, stable flies, fleas, any number of dung beetles, and other species suited to life in damp timber structures. From the occurrence of their bones, we may imagine that the rodent population made up of house mice and rats was large *(62)*. Rather than the brown variety (Latin, *Rattus norvegicus*) common today, however, the rats would have been the black species (Latin, *Rattus rattus*) which is almost extinct in Britain today. In medieval times its fleas are thought to have carried bubonic plague, most notoriously as the medieval Black Death, and one may wonder whether the disease had also been rife in Roman times.

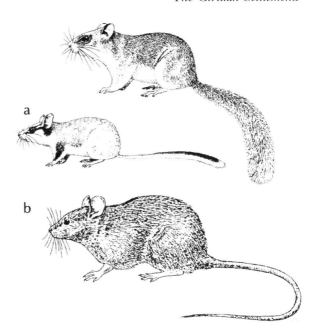

62 Rodents of Roman York:
a) the garden dormouse (*Eliomys quercinus*) with the edible dormouse (*Glis glis*) shown (top) for comparison; *b)* the black rat (*Rattus rattus*).

In any event, the ecological evidence from the General Accident site does cast a rather new light on conditions which might, on occasions, prevail in Roman towns, traditionally thought to have been models of order and cleanliness. It is difficult to know, however, if the site was in any way typical, as waterlogged ground conditions which preserve organic matter are so rare. Even in a York context it is possible that the squalor was purely localised and a product of the refuse-tipping habits of a restricted section of the community at a particular period of time.

THE PUBLIC BUILDINGS

One indication that environmental conditions at the General Accident site in the late second century were unusual and, in due course, considered by the authorities to be undesirable is that in the early third century there was a marked change in the character of occupation. The timber buildings were deliberately demolished and there was then an episode of levelling-up prior to the construction of a considerable stone structure. Its walls had unfortunately been completely demolished and its floors greatly disturbed by post-Roman activity, but the substantial nature of the foundations suggests that this was a major public building. It may even have been part of the same structure as that observed a little to the south-west in 1901, said to have had a 'gritstone façade'. One reason for reconstruction was perhaps that the manufacturing activities hitherto practised in this area were now considered unduly dangerous or noisome, and were moved to some less central location, but the change may also be to do with the town's acquisition of the status of *colonia* and provincial capital, which would have demanded a measure of architectural grandeur.

The location of the forum, the centre of civic life for both town and province, is unknown, although it probably lay close to the main road from the south-west. An altar dedicated to the spirit of the emperor linked to that of the *genius* of *Eboracum* found in George Hudson Street not far from the General Accident site would have been appropriate for the shrine (*aedes*) in a forum basilica. However, no certain structural remains have yet come to light in the area, although in 1898 almost opposite the site, Roman column bases in two rows 12m (40ft) apart were recorded (Site 12 on *44*). In one row seven bases survived and in the other four. In each row the column-to-column distance was 1.80m (6ft). This does not seem great enough for a forum basilica and it is more likely that these column bases belonged to some other building, possibly a temple. In the largely imaginative reconstruction illustration of Roman York *(colour plate 8)*, the forum is placed on a site south-west of these column bases and, although conjectural, this would at least have given the building a prominent and commanding site on rising ground. A little further to the south-west the corner of what must have been another substantial building was found (at the former Kenning's Garage, Micklegate, Site 13 on *44*) close to the main road from the south-west. This took the form of a foundation about 1m (3ft 3in) wide and 1.5m (5ft) deep. Oddly enough the structure did not adopt the road alignment but was on north-south and east-west axes. It is shown as a temple in the illustration.

Another site in the centre of the Roman town which has produced substantial building remains is 1-9 Micklegate (the former Queen's Hotel), excavated in 1988-9 (Site 20 on *44*; *63-4*). Unfortunately, due to problems of access and funding full excavation in advance of redevelopment was not possible and only a small part of the Roman building remains on the site was excavated. It is evident, however, that in the early third century an extensive stone structure, probably a bath house, succeeded an earlier, more modest building, itself pre-dated by a mid to late second-century episode of ditch-digging and rubbish-dumping. Two major walls built of oolitic limestone were recorded in detail, each of which was about 2.2m (7ft) thick. This is about as thick as Roman walls get in York. They survived to a height of up to 3.5m (11ft 6in) of which some 1.5m (5ft) had been below-ground footings. Both walls had brick-lined arched openings in them forming part of a hypocaust system which would have allowed hot air to circulate below a floor, presumably supported on *pilae*. Original floor level corresponded more or less to that of the top of the surviving walls before being lowered in the late Roman period (see p.149).

The search for Roman York's public buildings may now take us back to the north-western part of the *colonia*, where structural remains have been

63 1-9 Micklegate: Walls in a bath house of the early third century (looking south-west, 2m scale) showing the brick-lined arches – blocked in the fourth century – of the hypocaust system and the capping for a drain passing through the principal wall (lower left). Original floor level was at the top of the walls

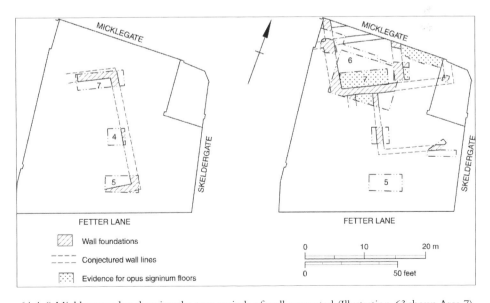

MICKLEGATE

SKELDERGATE

FETTER LANE

MICKLEGATE

SKELDERGATE

FETTER LANE

Wall foundations

Conjectured wall lines

Evidence for opus signinum floors

0   10   20 m

0   50 feet

64 1-9 Micklegate: plan showing the two periods of wall excavated (Illustration *63* shows Area 7)

found indicating the presence of another bath house. Unfortunately, little detail is known as they were unearthed either during the construction of the Old Station in 1839 or of the Air Raid Control Centre a century later. However, there were clearly two or more phases of building. The first consisted of relatively small structures, including three cold plunge-baths. Of a later date was an apsed *caldarium* 9m (30ft) wide and at least 10.5m (34ft) long which, for sheer size, is almost unparalleled in Britain. Other discoveries in the area indicate the presence of temples to the gods Serapis and Mithras (see below).

Finally, it has become clear that monumental buildings south-west of the Ouse were not confined to the town within the assumed line of its defences. At the site already referred to (p.50) on the north-west side of Blossom Street (Site 13 on *1*; observed in 1994) a very substantial wall foundation 1.5m (5 ft) thick, set at right angles to the main road from the south-west, was found. The function of the structure, of which this and some other stone walls found at the site formed part, is unknown, but it must have dominated the approach to the town.

All the buildings described in this section and elsewhere in this book are, of course, known only from archaeological work as there are no contemporary

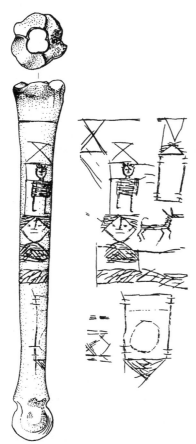

65 General Accident, Tanner Row: sheep tibia with incised representations of human figure, dog and building façades (length 120mm)

descriptions, but at this point we should note that York has produced what may be a most remarkable contemporary illustration, albeit very schematic, of a Roman street scene *(65)*. It was found scratched on a sheep bone and appears to show a human figure, a dog and some gabled facades. Although it appears child-like it may be a genuine attempt by someone, child or adult, to depict the city in which he or she lived some 1800 years ago.

RELIGION IN THE CIVILIAN SETTLEMENTS

The crudely scratched façades on the bone just described may perhaps be intended to represent temples, and it is clear that the religious practices of the townspeople at York were as diverse as those of the soldiers. Classical deities were worshipped alongside those of native origin such as Arciacus, referred to on an altar found near St Denys Church in Walmgate east of the river Foss but nowhere else, suggesting his cult was purely local.

Empire-wide, however, was the cult of the emperor, dedications to which we have already noted from Nessgate, north-east of the Ouse (p.88), and George Hudson Street (p.109). The cult would have been serviced by the *seviri augustales* ('six men of the emperor'), usually wealthy freedmen who nominally owed their freedom to their ultimate master, the emperor, and often took his family name as their own. We know of two *seviri* from York, one of whom was Marcus Aurelius Lunaris (p.83) and the other Verecundius Diogenes. The latter's name appeared on a coffin, now sadly lost, although surviving illustrations show an inscription giving his place of origin as what is now Bourges in northern France. Remarkably, the coffin of his wife survives and bears an inscription naming her as Julia Fortunata from Sardinia. The pair epitomise the cosmopolitan nature of the upper classes of the Roman *colonia* at York at the peak of its prosperity and self-confidence.

Like many other major Roman towns in Britain and elsewhere, York was a centre for several of the religious cults which, largely as a result of the movement of soldiers and merchants, swept through the western empire from the east in the second and third centuries. They included the cult of Cybele, a great mother goddess with fertility powers. She originated in Asia Minor, but had reached Rome as early as 191 BC, where her festivals were celebrated with extravagant and noisy ceremonies. An important part of the mythology associated with Cybele was the story of the shepherd boy Atys, probably depicted on a fragment of a tomb monument from York found on the Mount. He was Cybele's paramour who castrated himself in remorse for his infidelity with a nymph and in one version of the myth was turned into a pine tree. Priests of the cult, known as *galli*, were themselves eunuchs who ritually castrated themselves to show their devotion to the goddess.

Some of the new eastern cults were rather different in character to those associated with traditional Roman or native British religion. They claimed to offer adherents a more intimate relationship with a deity and access to revelations of secret knowledge ('mysteries') guaranteeing spiritual renewal and eternal life. Whereas Roman religious ceremonies had usually been held in public and were open to all comers, these 'mystery cults', as they are sometimes referred to, demanded membership of an exclusive group governed by rites of initiation.

Mystery cults practised in York included those dedicated to Isis and Mithras. Worship of the goddess Isis originated in Egypt and a temple dedicated to Serapis, her consort, apparently stood, as already noted, near the baths in the north-western part of the town. A fine inscribed tablet *(3)* commemorates the temple's construction by the legionary legate, Claudius Hieronymianus, whose second name suggests he was himself Egyptian. The central myth concerned the goddess herself, Serapis, and their son Harpokrates. Serapis was killed by the evil god Seth, but on achieving manhood Harpokrates defeated Seth and avenged the death of his father, who was then restored to life by Isis.

The cult of Mithras also concerned itself with rebirth, offering its adherents a spiritual journey from the darkness of death to the light of everlasting life.

66 Statue of Arimanius, the devil in Mithraic belief, dedicated by Volusius Ireneus who paid his vow willingly and deservedly – V(OTUM) [S](OLVENS) L(IBENS) M(ERITO). (Height 0.61m)

The central myth involved the sacrifice of a great bull which had been created at the beginning of time. This sacrifice is known as the tauroctony and can be seen on the Mithraic relief found on Micklegate, which suggests the presence of a temple in the heart of the *colonia (3)*. From the blood of the bull came all life and so an apparent act of destruction was transformed into one of creation. Mithras was opposed by the evil god Arimanius, who is represented on an altar from York found in 1874 while making an arch in the medieval city wall for Station Road *(66)*. This, the only depiction of Arimanius known from Britain, shows him as a winged figure, naked except for a fringed loin cloth tied with a knotted snake, symbolising the tortuous course of both the sun through the sky and of the initiate to revelation. He also carries the keys of heaven and a sceptre to symbolise his power. Mithras, 'also a soldier' as Rudyard Kipling describes him in *Puck of Pook's Hill*, was particularly revered by the upper echelons of the Roman army and merchant class, but the cult did not accept women or the lower orders and it appears to have declined in popularity in the fourth century.

HOUSES AND HOMES

It is entirely appropriate that the Roman altar from Bishophill (p.15) should refer to the 'gods of hospitality and home' as it was found in a residential zone of the *colonia* located south-east of the public buildings. The earliest activity recorded in this area dates to the mid to late second century when, for example, a street excavated at 58-9 Skeldergate was laid out close to the river front. Another street probably of similar date, running north-east/south-west (and therefore parallel to the main Roman approach road from the south-west) was found on a site in Bishophill Junior (Site 22 on *44*). Nearby at the St Mary Bishophill Senior site a late second-century building was found associated with metalworking. At this time it was on the periphery of the settlement, but in the early third century a major change to the topography of the area took place when the steep-sloping valley side was terraced to create a level plat-form for buildings. The full extent of the terrace is uncertain, but it may have been 200-300m (220–330 yards) long and was clearly a massive undertaking requiring the movement of thousands of tons of material and mobilisation of a considerable amount of labour. A street, which cannot be dated, found in Trinity Lane probably ran along the top (south-west side) of the terrace linking the buildings to the main road from the south-west.

   Extensive but poorly preserved remains of stone-built structures on the terrace have been excavated at 37 Bishophill Senior and St Mary Bishophill Senior, which were presumably domestic residences of some pretension. There was evidence for underfloor heating (hypocausts), decorative wall plas-ter and marble veneers. Fragmentary remains of other buildings have been found on a number of small sites on Bishophill Junior and Bishophill Senior. Another house, erected in the early third century, of which three rooms were excavated in 1976-7, was found at Clementhorpe, a little to the south-east of the assumed defences of the *colonia*. Its position would have afforded the owners pleasant views over the river Ouse to what, in Roman times, was probably open country beyond (Site 15 on *1; 75*).

In addition to any internal appointments and decorations, civilised living in the Roman houses of York depended on a good water supply. The Wellington Row site has already demonstrated that some parts of the settlement had piped water (pp.93-4) and further evidence for this takes the form of a remarkable stone fountain found in Bishophill in 1906 – now sadly dismantled *(67)*. It consisted of a tank about 1.15m (3ft 9in) square and 1m (3ft 3in) high, made of slabs of magnesian limestone bound with iron straps and held together with *opus signinum*. The back slab rose a further 220mm (8in) and was pierced by an inlet which would have been connected to the public water supply. It would have been in keeping with the Roman preference for using gravity to move water around that there was a distribution centre at a high point in the *colonia* from where it was piped to fountains, baths and selected houses. As in the Roman fortress, however, piped water would have been supplemented by wells, and a very fine timber-lined example some 6m (20ft) deep was excavated at 58-9 Skeldergate *(68)*. Water was not only needed for drinking but also for gardens, and in the Skeldergate well there were clippings of box, much favoured by the Romans for hedges. Box not only looks good in a formal setting, but is pleasantly aromatic and was thought to have curative properties.

THE PEOPLE OF THE TOWN

The inhabitants of the agreeable south-eastern part of the *colonia* and areas immediately outside it, which not only offered views over the Ouse but also a retreat from the bustle, noise and smells of the public buildings and riverside quays, are of course largely unknown to us as individuals. We may imagine, however, that numbered amongst the more prosperous were some of those people whose names have survived on inscribed funerary monuments. In total there are nineteen tombstones and eight sarcophagi from York on which the inscriptions give the names of the deceased (in the cases of four of the tombstones there are two names). In addition eighteen other names appear, being those of the people who had the tombstone or sarcophagus set up. Most of the funerary monuments from York probably date to the late second to early third century, a period when there was a particular vogue for commemorating the dead in stone throughout the empire. As we have already seen, the men referred to in inscriptions include civic officials, legionary veterans and

67 (above) The stone street fountain from Bishophill Junior (height 1m)

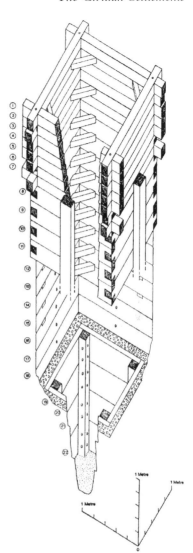

68 (right) 58-9 Skeldergate: an axonometric reconstruction of a timber-lined well showing forms of joint.
Tiers 1-7 saddle-jointed (excluding tier 6 – half lap)
with corner braces and external retaining posts; tiers
8-18 dove-tail jointed (16-18 without braces); tiers
19-22 inset with internal corner posts

merchants, but they also had families, and York has a number of inscriptions
which refer to women and children.

One of York's finest Roman tombstones is that of Julia Velva *(colour plate
10)*. Above the inscribed panel is carved a family dining scene where Julia
Velva herself reclines on a couch standing in a semi-circular headed niche
intended to portray part of the dining room of a smart town house. This room
was known in Latin as a *triclinium*, meaning that it afforded space for three
couches. In the Roman world it was considered the height of good manners to
dine while reclining. Only the servants, who took the food to their master and
mistress, and the children sat at table. To the right of Julia Velva as we look
at her stands a booted male figure, who is presumably Aurelius Mercurialis

named in the inscription as her heir. He, we are told, had the tombstone 'set up for himself and his family whilst he was alive'. Mercurialis may also have been Julia Velva's husband, but this is not made clear. To the left of the dining scene there is a girl seated holding a pet bird. A male figure stands in the centre; he is probably a slave, shown in typical Roman style as a small person because of his inferior status. There is also a table set with dishes of food which may symbolise the sort of funeral banquet which would have taken place after the burial of an individual from a wealthy family. As well as being a memorial for Julia Velva, this tombstone is a status symbol demonstrating the wealth and standing of a leading York family and showing them self-confidently facing the world in what would, in fact, have been a semi-public room in their house where clients were received and patronage dispensed. In origin the tombstone would, as was usual in Roman times, have been painted, making its impact on the viewer all the more forceful. The inscription tells us that Julia Velva died aged 50 years and that she was 'most dutiful' (rendered as PIENTISSIME); this is a good example of the sort of epithet Roman women were often given on their tombstones – whether justified or not we cannot tell!

Another insight into people's lives in Roman York is provided by the inscription on the sarcophagus of Aelia Severa, wife of Caecilius Rufus who had pre-deceased her *(69)*. She is referred to as a member of the *honestiores*, and this serves to make the point that even after Caracalla's extension of citizenship in 212 Roman society remained as hierarchical as ever. The *honestiores* formed the upper crust of citizens occupying positions of importance in government and administration and enjoying wide-ranging privileges while the mass of the population, known as the *humiliores*, remained very much second-class.

69 The sarcophagus of Aelia Severa, a lady of the upper classes, the *honestiores* – HONESTE FEMINE – once the wife of Caecilius Rufus. She lived 27 years, 9 months and 4 days – V(IXIT) AN(NOS) XXVII M(ENSES) VIII D(IES) IIII. The sarcophagus was set in place by Caecilius Musicus, freedman – LIB(ERTVS). Found in 1859 in Dalton Terrace

70 (left) Relief of a smith, probably a representation of the god Vulcan, found at Dringhouses in 1860 (height 1.32m)

71 (right) Tombstone of Julia Brica, aged 31, and her daughter Sempronia Martina, aged 6, set up by Sempronius Martinus. Julia Brica holds an urn and her daughter a bird. Found in 1892 on The Mount (height 1.78m)

The inscription on Aelia Severa's coffin also tells us that it was paid for by Caecilius Musicus, a freed slave (*libertus*) who had evidently taken his master's family name on receiving his freedom, and we might guess from his familiar name, Musicus, that his job as a slave had been as household musician. On the death of his former mistress we may imagine that Musicus inherited the family fortune and became a member of the local *nouveau riche*.

On only a small number of York's Roman tombstones are there actual representations of the deceased as on that of Julia Velva, but they are invaluable for giving us an impression of the appearance of people in Roman York. Some men are shown wearing a cloak which came down to their knees over a short tunic tied at the waist, although Aurelius Mercurialis on Julia Velva's tombstone *(colour plate 10)* has a mantle over his shoulders tied like a scarf. A more unusual item of male clothing is worn by a blacksmith, probably the god Vulcan, depicted in relief on a monument from Dringhouses

(70). This is a so-called *exomis*, a short tunic which leaves one shoulder bare. Representative of Roman women in York is Julia Brica *(71)*, who is shown dressed in a long under-tunic below a shorter knee-length tunic tied at the waist with a mantle over her shoulders.

Roman hair styles shown on tombstones mostly represent late second- to early third-century styles. Men were usually, like the emperors, bearded and moustached. Women, such as Julia Velva or Julia Brica, often have a central parting with the hair waved and swept back probably into a bun or chignon.

There are six children shown on York tombstones. Alongside Julia Brica is her daughter Sempronia Martina, who died at the age of six. She is dressed very like her mother and there does not seem to have been a great deal of difference between the clothing worn by adults and that worn by children in Roman times. A distinctive feature of the children on tombstones, however, is that they appear to hold items symbolising childhood. For example, both Martina and the girl on Julia Velva's tombstone hold birds, probably pets, and other children are shown with balls.

In an era of little medical knowledge infant mortality was high, and sad testimony to this is also provided by Candida Barita's tombstone, which records that she was accompanied to the 'divine shades' by her two little daughters Mantia and Tetrica. The most touching testimony to the devotion of local people to their children is, however, the tombstone of little Corellia Optata, who was mourned by her father in a verse epitaph translated by RCHME as follows:

> To the spirits of the departed, Corellia Optata, 13 years old. Ye hidden spirits that dwell in Pluto's Acherusian realms, whom the scanty ash and the shade, the body's image, seek after life's little day, I, the pitiable father of an innocent daughter, caught by cheating hope, lament her final end. Quintus Corellius Fortis, the father had this made.

THE CEMETERIES OF ROMAN YORK

Reference to what the funerary monuments can tell us about certain individual residents of Roman York may now be followed by an examination of the cemeteries in which not only were these monuments to the wealthy set up, but much of the population found its last resting place. One of the greatest changes in social customs introduced to northern Britain by the Romans was burial of the dead. Although there had been a tradition of burial amongst the Parisi of east Yorkshire, members of the pre-Roman Iron Age population in the rest of the north were rarely buried. Some other way of disposing of their bodies which leaves no archaeological trace must have been employed. One possibility is excarnation, which involves exposing the dead to the elements.

The Romans, however, usually buried their dead and, according to their laws, burial had to take place outside areas inhabited by the living. Typically, Roman cemeteries lined the main roads as they approached forts, towns and other settlements, allowing passers-by to pay due respect to the dead and keep their memory green *(colour plate 9)*.

The cemeteries of Roman York were largely unearthed in the nineteenth century and were not well recorded. Compared to some other Roman towns in Britain, few burials have been systematically excavated, but some patterns in the overall development of York's cemeteries are, however, apparent. As far as the details of burial customs and practice are concerned, the York evidence suggests great variety. This is only to be expected in a place which was throughout the Roman period home to people of diverse geographical origins whose status in society ranged from the highest ranks of the Roman government and military establishment to the humblest of slaves.

The distribution of cremation burials may be taken to give some indication of the location of early Roman cemeteries at York because it is assumed that cremation was, until the mid-second century, the preferred, if not exclusive rite for the disposal of the deceased (except for infants). When evidence for cremation burials is plotted it appears that the cemeteries were usually close to the main approach roads to the fortress and other settled areas, but often at some distance from them. Cemeteries at Burton Stone Lane and Clifton Fields, for example, are about 0.7km (⅓ mile) north-west of the fortress while two cemeteries at Heworth are 0.85km (½ mile) north-east of the fortress and another at Fishergate is about 1km (¾ mile) south-east of it. Fifty-three cremations probably dating from about the year 160 onwards were found at Trentholme Drive, the largest Roman cemetery area excavated archaeologically in York, which was close to the line of the main approach road from the south-west and over 1km (¾ mile) from the river Ouse. Of particular interest at Trentholme Drive was a stone structure surrounded by a dense layer of charcoal, which was interpreted as an *ustrina*, the place where the cremation process itself took place. It appears that the body of the deceased was usually burnt on a wooden bier and offerings might be made during the burning process. The charred remains of the body were interred in some sort of container, usually made of pottery, but glass jars and lead canisters are also known from York.

Cremation fell out of favour in the later second century, although it was still used in elite social circles until the early third century as in the case of the emperor Septimius Severus himself (p.80). Cremation was replaced by burial of the dead unburnt, as what archaeologists usually refer to as 'inhumation'. For periods in which inhumation was standard practice, the pattern of cemetery development at York becomes difficult to trace in any detail. It is clear, however, that in the second half of the second century and third century some very large cemeteries emerged. The Trentholme Drive excavations produced some 342 inhumations dating from the mid-second century to the early fourth, but this site was only part of a cemetery which lined the main Roman road from the south-west. Elsewhere on the south-west bank of the Ouse another major cemetery developed on the site of what is now the Railway Station, around a Roman road which approached the *colonia* from the north-west. Burials have also been found in the south-eastern part of what had probably, by the third century, been incorporated into the *colonia*, and outside it in the Clementhorpe and Bishopgate Street area. North-east of the Ouse, cemeteries lay either side of the approach road from the north-west in the Bootham and Clifton areas. In addition, small groups of burials or even isolated individuals have been found on what were presumably vacant plots of land in many parts of the immediate York area.

Within the cemeteries there would probably have been distinct plots owned by families or other social groups. Evidence from elsewhere in the Roman world suggests that the rich and powerful usually strove to secure plots in prominent locations close to the roads, where their monuments reminded visitors and locals alike of who the most important people in the community were. It is no surprise, therefore, that at York many of the inscribed stone funerary monuments have been found close to the main road from the south-west. Julia Velva's tombstone, for example, would have stood in a very prominent position near a local high point where, today, The Mount is joined by Albemarle Road. The Trentholme Drive cemetery area at the bottom of the hill to the south-west of this location and close to the marshy ground (still commemorated in the name of the Knavesmire nearby) may, because of its less favoured location, have contained for the most part humbler members of the community.

Inhumation graves were usually simple bath-shaped pits, but iron nails surviving in them show that the bodies were frequently interred in wooden coffins. Lead and stone coffins (sarcophagi) are also known *(28 and 69)*, but they were expensive items and would normally have been restricted to the richer families. On occasions, to judge by presence of inscriptions as in the cases of Aurelius Super (see p.60-1) and Aelia Severa (p.118), sarcophagi were not buried, but placed above ground in a mausoleum, although the mausolea in York are unlikely to have been as elaborate as some of those still visible today outside Rome and other Mediterranean cities. The demolished remains of a small mausoleum of early third-century date was found at 35-41 Blossom Street, another site close to the approach road from the south-west. It had been a stone structure with a square ground plan measuring 6m x 6m (20ft x 20ft). The walls were plastered and the floor was of *opus signinum*. A woman of about 40-50 years and a juvenile had been buried on a north-east/south-west alignment within the structure and other burials with a similar alignment were made nearby. The structure may have been covered by a tunnel-vault similar to that which still survives covering a stone coffin in a small mausoleum in the cellar

72 Tile tombs (from C. Wellbeloved, 1842. Eburacum)

of 104 The Mount. A humbler version of these stone-built mausolea, of which several examples are known, took the form of a sort of box made entirely of tiles *(72)*.

In the absence of a permanent structure, grave markers would have been necessary to preserve order in cemeteries, but as we have already seen (p.116) tombstones were rare. Simple mounds of earth or wooden posts may have been used in most cases but were, of course, not permanent and have not been recorded in excavation. Another reason for identifying Trentholme Drive as a cemetery of people of low status was its apparent lack of permanent grave markers. This may have contributed to a marked lack of order, with graves lying on a variety of different alignments and frequently cutting into one another.

In at least some cases bodies were probably buried clothed, although all that usually survives are jewellery items such as rings and bracelets and occasionally the iron hobnails of boots and shoes. Other objects, grave goods as they are usually called, were sometimes included in both cremation and inhumation graves. Pottery vessels were the most common grave goods and may originally have contained food either to provide nourishment for the deceased's journey to the spirit world or to symbolise participation with the living in a funeral meal. More unusual grave goods include a fan with ivory handles found with a burial in a stone coffin in the Railway Station cemetery and a figurine of Hercules with his club from a burial north-east of the Ouse near Peasholme Green.

Views on the afterlife in the Roman world were diverse. There is not the space to discuss them in detail here, but there is some evidence from burials and funerary monuments for the importation of traditional Roman ideas to York. The standard dedication DM (*dis manibus*) in funerary inscriptions suggests a belief that the dead were to be commended to divine care in the next world. One version of this world, ultimately of Greek origin, is described by Lucian of Samosata (Syria) writing in about the year 160. In a satirical account of traditional religion he tells us that it was thought that the dead travelled to an underworld beyond the river Styx (sometimes known as Acheron) in the care of the ferryman Charon. On the other side, having passed the ferocious multi-headed dog Cerberus, they would find themselves where Hades/Pluto, brother of Zeus/Jupiter, presided. Fortunate souls might in due course make their way to Lethe, the fountain or river of forgetfulness, and then pass on to the Elysian Fields before being reborn. A second group wandered lonely as shadows for ever more. Those least fortunate were persecuted by the furies. Explicit evidence from York for these ideas is to be found in Corellia Optata's epitaph (see p.120) with its reference to Pluto's Acherusian realms. In addition, there are examples of coins buried with the dead which may have been intended as payment for the ferryman. For example, the skeleton of a woman buried in the late second century, shown in *colour plate 18*, was found with a coin (of Faustina II, wife of Marcus Aurelius) in her mouth, as well as a pair of silver finger rings, a lamp and three pots.

As far as archaeologists are concerned, one of the most valuable aspects of excavating burials is that they give an insight into the physical characteristics of ancient populations. Examination of a human skeleton can allow an expert to determine, first of all, the deceased individual's sex, approximate age at death and stature. In addition, certain types of wound, notably limb fractures, as well as certain diseases and congenital disorders may be revealed, although it is rarely possible to identify the cause of death. To get a reliable picture of a population as a whole, however, it is necessary to examine a large number of bodies and compare them one with another. This is why the Trentholme Drive site is so important. Although techniques of analysis have advanced considerably since the 1960s when Dr Warwick studied the skeletons, it remains striking that, of those whose sex could be identified, there were four times as many males as females. Town cemeteries usually contain a roughly equal number of men and women, and there is no ready explanation for the anomaly unless the data reflect York's status as an army base.

As we have already noted, life expectancy in Roman times was low compared to today. Infant mortality was particularly high *(74 and 78)*, although few very young individuals were found at Trentholme Drive, perhaps because the bones had not survived in the ground. Once infancy had been passed, life expectancy remained low in modern terms with as much as 75-80% of the population dying before the age of about 40. In *73* the data on age at death

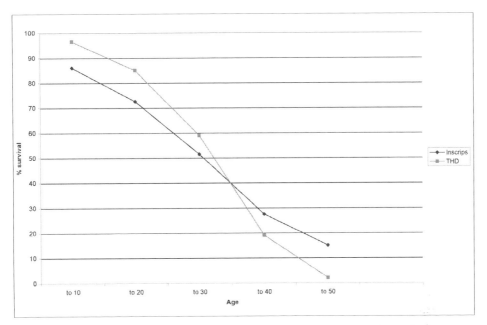

73 Graph showing percentage of people alive at successive ages up to 50 for those whose ages are given on Roman funerary monuments from Britain (222 recorded up to end of 1954 in R.G. Collingwood and R.P. Wright, *The Roman Inscriptions of Britain* I, 1965) and for population at Trentholme Drive cemetery, York (290 aged by R. Warwick in L.P. Wenham, *The Romano-British Cemetery at Trentholme Drive, York*, 1968)

74 Infant skeleton in a lead-lined coffin from the County Hospital-Foss Bank site, north-east of the fortress (scale 0.5m). The white squares indicate the location of coffin nails

from Trentholme Drive are shown alongside those from all the inscribed Roman tombstones from Britain (recorded up to the end of 1954) which give an age at death. Although there are doubts about the reliability of the inscription evidence, the two groups present a remarkably similar picture. The only people apparently missing at Trentholme Drive are the very old.

When the stature of the skeletons is considered, it appears that the men from Trentholme Drive were on average 1.7m (5ft 7in) tall and women 1.55m (5ft 1in). Contrary to popular belief about people in the past being much smaller than they are today these figures remained more or less unchanged in the British population until the Second World War, although since then there has been a slight rise in the averages due to better nutrition. As in most ancient populations there was considerable evidence for wear and tear on the bones of the Trentholme Drive skeletons and evidence for arthritis was common in the over thirties. There has been little published material on Roman human remains from York since Dr Warwick's work on Trentholme Drive, but there are now sufficient skeletons from recent excavations to make a comparative study with those from Trentholme Drive a valid and much needed exercise.

ROMAN YORK IN ITS REGION

Immediately outside the core settled areas of Roman York south-west of the Ouse, there is, as in those areas themselves, evidence for an increased level of activity from the late second century onwards. In zones not occupied by cemeteries this took the form of the laying out of some new roads and the division of the land with 'field ditches' very similar to those recorded north-east of the Ouse (p.89). Settlement in the sense of buildings appears, however, to be confined to areas close to the presumed *colonia* defences or to the approach roads. The evidence from Blossom Street on the main road from the south-west has already been noted, but about 3.25km (2 miles) south-west of the centre of York, again on the line of the road, evidence has come to light for Roman occupation in Dringhouses, now a suburb of the city. Timber structures, cobbled surfaces and ditches may be set alongside a number of burials to suggest the existence of a roadside settlement of the second to third century. Work in 2003 at the former Starting Gate pub (Site 16 on *1*) revealed the walls of what may have been a second-century Roman predecessor, to judge by the large quantity of amphora and flagon fragments found.

A full discussion of how York may be set within the context of the region as a whole in the Roman period lies beyond the scope of this book, but as far as settlement is concerned, a number of general points may be made to show that York's development as described above was in many ways in keeping with regional trends. Whereas in the pre-Roman period there was little evidence for a hierarchy of settlement of any complexity, by about 50 years after the conquest the situation had clearly changed. Forts occupied for any length of time had begun to spawn what are usually known as *vici*, settlements under military supervision analogous to that growing up outside the fortress at York. Some of these *vici*, such as those at Catterick and Malton, appear by the third century to have taken on a life their own as what archaeologists often refer to as 'small towns' in recognition of their diverse economic and social functions. In addition, there were the regional capitals acting as centres of local government at Aldborough and Brough-on-Humber, which were probably founded in the early second century. At the same time there emerged other settlements along the lines of the main Roman roads which may have been more than simple villages but places with certain market and other functions. Recently investigated examples include Hayton and Shiptonthorpe about 25km (15 miles) south-east of York on the road to Brough.

In the countryside at a distance from the road lines it remains difficult to describe the history of Roman settlement in any detail, but there appears to be some evidence for change in the pattern of settlement location, land division and subsistence base in the later second or early third century, at least in certain areas such as the Wolds and Vale of York. Change is characterised, in part, by disappearance of settlements of pre-Roman origin, the replacement of small enclosures with larger ones and the appearance of deep wells and stone-built kilns about 5m (16ft 6in) long with T-shaped flues thought to be used for drying out cereal crops. These changes may have been connected to a new emphasis on arable agriculture as opposed to stock-rearing, as has been suggested for the immediate York area on the basis of the 'field ditches'. In some parts of the region, what was probably increased profitability of agriculture attendant on rising population and improved communications by road and water led to the emergence of villas. Although a word which is difficult to define exactly, a villa in Roman Britain is usually considered to be a house in a rural setting which was built largely of stone and which enjoyed such appointments as heated rooms, baths and mosaic floors. In the south of England villas had existed since the late first century, but they were much slower to appear in the north and there were never any establishments to compare with some of the great southern villas, like Bignor or Chedworth. This may, up to a point, indicate that the north was less productive agriculturally than the south, but also perhaps that the people here were rather less ready to absorb the Romanised cultural values which villas epitomise.

There is no evidence at present that York was, like some of the towns of Roman Britain, surrounded by villas. This may, to some extent, be because of the existence of the legionary *territorium* on which no independent landowners were able to settle. In addition, the local landowners may perhaps have been largely veterans and government officials, rather than native British aristocrats, who preferred to have their principal dwelling in or immediately outside the town. In 2003, excavations in Heslington about 3.5km (2 miles) east of the centre of York near to the main approach road from Brough-on Humber revealed a small bath house which may have been part of an as yet undiscovered villa complex. However, at present the nearest certain villa to York appears to be at Wilstrop Hall, Green Hammerton, 11km (6½ miles) to the west, where a bath house was found in 1975. Another may have been located at Kirkby Wharfe 18km (11 miles) to the south-west, but the most extensively excavated in the York region was at Dalton Parlours 20km (12 miles) to the south-west of York and 4km (2½ miles) south of Wetherby. It stood on the well-drained fertile soils of the magnesian limestone belt which runs north-south between the Pennines to the west and the clay of the Vale of York to the east. The origins of Dalton Parlours as a settlement lay in the pre-Roman Iron Age, but the first stone building of the villa probably dates to the late second or early third century. In addition to Dalton Parlours, there were a number of other villas on the west side of York, including two more on the magnesian limestone at Castle Dykes, North Stainley and at Well, both near Ripon. Another suitable area for agriculture in the region was Ryedale, north of York, where a villa was discovered at Hovingham in the nineteenth century. A sequence similar to that at Dalton Parlours, with a native farm developing into a villa by the later second or early third century, can be found on sites to the north-east and east of York, including a number occupying favourable spots on the Wolds at Harpham, Langton and Rudston.

THE CIVILIAN SETTLEMENTS AT YORK: THE STORY SO FAR

In the first edition of this book the concluding section of this chapter was entitled 'The civilian settlements at York: success or failure?'. This led me to ask whether the Roman town at York after the reign of Septimius Severus could, in more favourable economic and political circumstances than those generally thought to have prevailed in the mid-third century, have become as large as some of the other towns of Roman Britain such as Canterbury, Cirencester and, notably, London or even the larger Gallic cities like Lyon or Trier. I calculated that the area within the presumed Roman defences on the south-west bank of the Ouse was about 27ha (67 acres). If core civilian areas north-east of the Ouse were added, this might have reached about 40ha (99 acres). By comparison, the walled area of Roman London was 140ha (346 acres) and that of Trier some 200ha (500 acres). It would be surprising if Roman York ever had more than 3,000 civilian inhabitants, while London may have come close to 10,000 at its height and Trier twice that number. In other words, I was asking whether York, which had become an urban place at a rather later date than most in Roman Britain, had suffered from arrested development.

Since the first edition, however, it has become clear that my questions may have been based on something of a false premise in that, while the authority of government in the west did appear to weaken markedly following the death in 235 of Severus Alexander, the last of the Severi, and the economy to suffer from worsening inflation and other ills, one cannot really identify a matching decline in York's fortunes between the reigns of Severus and Constantine. While the deposition of broken pottery sherds cannot be treated as an infallible guide, it is nonetheless striking that Jason Monaghan's survey of almost 200 sites shows that, compared to the quantity recovered which can be ascribed to the second-early third century, there is no evidence for any diminution in quantity ascribable to the mid- to late third century, or to the first half of the fourth century for that matter. In addition new buildings, for example at Coppergate north–east of the Ouse (pp.88-9), were apparently erected in the mid-third century. What may represent the bucking of a trend to stagnation seen in other urban places in Britain was probably due to York's role in servicing the needs of the army and the newly created provincial government, and to a continuing role as a regional market centre to which agricultural products were sent and from which goods such as pottery, glassware and wine landed at the port of York were distributed.

If one were to sum up the character of mid-third-century York as we understand it in 2003, one might begin by saying that on both sides of the river Ouse there were clearly buildings of some size and architectural pretension, and some of the amenities of a classical city, if modest by Mediterranean standards. The civilian population was varied in its occupations, and included craftsmen and merchants as well as retired legionaries and members of the Roman governing class. We also know that, although the population may have been largely of native British stock, many of their number were drawn from other parts of the empire. Amongst the leading families of the community, moreover, there was the wealth to indulge in sophisticated Romanised tastes in a variety of commodities ranging from food to tombstones. All things considered, it may be suggested that York had a cosmopolitan atmosphere quite different from that of the nearby *civitas* capital at Aldborough or indeed of any other Roman town in Britain except the provincial capital at London.

By way of giving the reader something of a visual impression of the character and layout of mid-third-century York, I have chosen to conclude this chapter by drawing attention to the reconstruction illustration *(colour plate 8)*. This is based on archaeological evidence where possible, but a good deal of the detail is, it may be freely admitted, a product of the imagination albeit, one would hope, an informed imagination. At the top of the view is a part of the legionary fortress with the headquarters building, bath house and barracks in their correct locations. I have shown the defences as I believe they would have appeared with the projecting towers on the south-west front (see pp.71-4). Areas south-east and south-west of the fortress I have shown as fairly densely built-up around the streets of which the lines are known. South-west of the

Ouse the civilian settlement is shown focused on the main road from the south-west, aligned more or less exactly north-east/south-west and within defences formed by stone walls. Other streets are shown largely as the excavated evidence suggests, adopting the same alignment. However, I have also shown that other alignments existed due either to constraints of the landscape or to historical circumstances. Firstly, in the south-east part of the town a street discovered at 58-9 Skeldergate running along the riverside was aligned north-north-west/ south-south-east, an alignment also adopted by one of the principal axes of the bath house at 1-9 Micklegate. Secondly, in the north-west part of the town (lower left) I have shown the legacy of probable early Roman buildings which apparently adopted an alignment at about 15° to the main road from the south-west. Between the streets I have tried to give some impression of the likely character of buildings based on the little that is known from York itself and on Roman towns elsewhere in Britain and the western empire. In short, I have tried to show what a town influenced by the principles of classical planning and monumentality set down on the banks of the Ouse might have looked like in its heyday.

CHAPTER 5

LATE ROMAN YORK

The altar dedicated at Bordeaux by Marcus Aurelius Lunaris in 237 *(43)* is the latest datable Roman inscription to refer to York and few, if any, of the undatable inscriptions from the city itself can be confidently given a later date. The absence of late Roman inscriptions from York and their scarcity country-wide is, however, just one indication of changes in cultural attitudes which accompanied changes in military, political and economic circumstances in the middle years of the third century throughout the western empire. After the death of the emperor Severus Alexander in 235 there was a long episode of internal weakness as rival claimants, each backed by sections of the army, vied for the imperial crown. In 233 and 258 there were serious attacks on Gaul and northern Italy by a Germanic people known as the Alamanni. Out of the chaos resulting from the collapse of the Rhineland frontier there emerged in 260 a breakaway 'Empire of the Gallic Provinces', which encompassed most of Gaul, Germany and Spain as well as Britain. It was initially ruled by the army commander Postumus, who succeeded in restoring the west's defences, but after his murder in 269 the Gallic Empire fell into the hands of less competent men and in 274 it collapsed, leaving the emperor Aurelian to restore unified rule from the centre.

It is not always easy to determine how these developments affected Roman Britain. Archaeological evidence for the mid-third century can be difficult to interpret because the import of samian pottery had more or less come to an end and the supply of coinage became intermittent, almost drying up at times. Without samian and coins it has often proved difficult to give exact dates to the excavated sequences which cover the period, although as far as York is concerned this has been largely overcome by Jason Monaghan's wide-ranging survey of pottery from the city referred to at the end of the last chapter. In general terms, however, it appears that Britain avoided the worst of the tur-moil afflicting the western empire and suffered no major invasions by way of either the coast or the northern land frontier. At the same time the effects of empire-wide inflation and the disruption of inter-provincial trade attendant on economic and political instability led to significant changes in the way Roman Britain functioned.

One of these changes was probably the development of a more self-sufficient economy in the province as a whole and in its regions. The best evidence for this is to be found in patterns of pottery production and supply, which probably reflect changing trade patterns in a more general sense. As far as York is concerned, there is a near absence of wares imported from outside Britain. At Wellington Row, where as we have already seen (p.107) 25-36% of pottery assemblages from the mid-second- to mid-third-century layers were made up of imports, deposits of the late third to fourth century produced only 5% and much of this was probably redeposited material, originally discarded in earlier periods. Pottery supply to York was now overwhelmingly local, and in the last quarter of the third century a number of important late Roman industries began production. For example, the wares made in the kilns at Crambeck, located between York and Malton, occur in large quantities in later Roman deposits. The only important source at any distance was the Nene Valley around Peterborough about 200km (120 miles) to the south.

What appears to be a revival in the fortunes of the western empire in the late third century must, to a large extent, have been due to a reassertion of governmental control at the centre which began during the rule of the emperor Diocletian (284-305). Running the empire at the best of times was an extremely taxing job for one man and so Diocletian established a system called the Tetrarchy, both to lessen the burden and provide for a more ordered succession. There were now four emperors, one senior (the Augustus) and one junior (the Caesar), for both the eastern and western halves of the empire. Diocletian also subdivided the provinces again. Britain had become two as a result of Caracalla's reform, but it now became four and a new tier of administration, the Diocese, was established. This was administered by an official known as the Vicar of Britain with his capital at London (now known as *Augusta*), who was in turn answerable to the Prefect of the Gauls in Trier. York remained a capital, but of a slightly smaller province than before, known as *Britannia Secunda*. In addition, at about the same time, control of the military and civilian spheres was separated so that the provincial governors were no longer in charge of troops. The new system was more bureaucratic than the old, but served to keep the western empire together for another 100 years or so.

In a political sense, Britain's situation in the late third century was complicated by a further secessionist episode as a result of the revolt in 285 of Carausius, a Roman naval commander. In 293 he was murdered by his successor Allectus, who was then defeated by Constantius, then the Caesar in the west, in 296. Some ten years later, while campaigning in the north, Constantius, by now the Augustus in the west, was to become the second emperor to die in York. On his death the Tetrarchy system demanded that the Caesar in the west, one Flavius Valerius Severus, should be promoted to Augustus. However, according to the fourth-century historian Aurelius Victor, Constantius's troops, urged on by Crocus, a king of the Alamanni who was serving with the Roman army in Britain, acclaimed his son Constantine as emperor. Over the next eighteen years Constantine gradually finished off his rivals and in 324 emerged as supreme ruler of the empire.

Constantine I 'the Great' is perhaps best known for tolerating Christianity and for making it an official religion of the Roman state. At the same time, paradoxical though it may seem, Constantine's reign saw worship of the emperor as a superhuman, if not divine, being reach new heights. We can get some flavour of this from the panegyrics (poems of praise) which were offered to the emperor on state occasions. One example, composed by the poet Eumenius, also shows how Britain, as the place where Constantine came to power, was able to bask in some reflected glory. 'Fortunate and happier than all lands, because she first saw Constantine Caesar' he wrote, and then goes on:

> Gracious gods! What means this, that always from some remote end of the world, new deities descend to be universally revered? Truly places nearer to heaven are more sacred than inland regions; and it was very proper that an emperor should be sent by the gods from the region [i.e. Britain] in which the earth terminates.

Another expression of the emperor's status which became popular in the fourth century was the larger-than-life monumental statue. A head taken to represent Constantine *(colour plate 11)* was found in Stonegate, York in the early nineteenth century and we may imagine that it came from a statue standing before or perhaps within the legionary headquarters.

With the exception of a stone building found at Hornpot Lane/Low Petergate (Site 13 on *13*), there is very little construction work in the fortress at York which can be ascribed to the early fourth century, but this may have been the time when an official known as the *Dux Britanniarum* (Duke of the Britains – meaning the provinces of Britain) was installed here. He is referred to in the *Notitia Dignitatum*, a list of official and military dispositions in the Roman empire probably dating to the early fifth century, but incorporating earlier material.

It is clear from the *Notitia Dignitatum* and other sources that the organisation of the Roman army in the fourth century had changed considerably since the early days of conquest. The first-century army had relied heavily on the legions attached to particular provinces and based on or near the frontiers. It was assumed that the empire would continue to expand and the legions would continue to move into forward positions. By the time of Constantine, however, the empire had long since ceased to expand and the army had adopted a defence-in-depth approach geared primarily to repelling invaders and making the frontiers secure. It was now found more useful to have a mobile field force, largely mounted, which could be moved to trouble spots as required. The frontiers themselves were manned by troops known as *limitanei*, who may be thought of as a militia raised from the local population. The *Notitia Dignitatum* suggests that military commanders now had responsibility for areas rather than specific bodies of men. The *Dux Britanniarum* was probably in charge of all troops in the north of Britain, whether they were detachments of the field army or the frontier guards. Although the *Notitia* states that York remained the base of a unit known as the Sixth Legion, it is impossible to know what its strength was in the time of Constantine and his successors.

LATE ROMAN HOUSES IN YORK

In the civilian settlements at York the most striking archaeological evidence for the late third or early fourth century takes the form of a number of substantial residences. Two examples found in the nineteenth century in the north-western quarter of the *colonia*, south-west of the Ouse, contained fine mosaics. They are taken to be products of a local school of mosaicists whose work is also known in Aldborough and in villas around Brough-on-Humber. Three pavements were discovered on Toft Green in 1853 (Site 5 on *44*), of which one has a design incorporating, at the corners, female busts representing the four seasons. Spring is symbolised by a swallow *(colour plate 12)*, summer by a bunch of grapes, autumn by a rake, and winter by a bare bough. The seasons are a common theme on British mosaics, but of additional interest in this mosaic is the head of the gorgon Medusa in the centre. In Greek legend Medusa's ghastly face turned all who gazed upon it to stone. In many Roman representations, as on the Toft Green mosaic and on the jet medallions from York, her face was made conventionally female with only the odd wild locks of

75 Clementhorpe: view to the east of the remains of a large house of the early third century to which an apse (foreground) was added in the early fourth century (2m scale). A room (upper left) has a mosaic pavement also of the early fourth century. The bath-shaped pits are graves of the medieval St Clement's nunnery

76 Clementhorpe: part of the early
fourth-century mosaic (1m scale)

hair to represent writhing snakes seen in more detailed depictions. Nevertheless
it would have been thought to attract and hold the powers of evil.

Part of another late Roman town house was found in 1961-3 north-west
of the medieval church of St Mary Bishophill Junior (Site 21 on *44*). Although
the walls had been heavily robbed, the building had probably been quite
extensive, with at least two ranges of rooms around a courtyard *(5)*. An apse
had been added to one wing during the life of the building, essentially as an
architectural flourish to enhance its appearance, and it may have been used
as the focus for a large *triclinium*. In the house partially excavated at St Mary
Bishophill Senior, an apse again formed part of the upgrading of a modest
earlier stone house which also acquired additional ranges around a courtyard.
In the range most extensively examined there were four rooms connected by
a corridor and three of them had underfloor heating supplied by a furnace
attached to the outside wall.

At Clementhorpe, immediately south-east of the presumed *colonia* enclosure, the principal room of the house described above (p.116) had an apse
added to it on the west side *(75* and *colour plate 13)*. Rather than being semi-
circular, however, it had a most unusual polygonal form. At this time the
room was also given painted plaster on the walls and a new floor. Only red
tesserae (small rectangular tiles) had survived around the edge of the room, but
they may have framed a mosaic in the centre. In an adjacent room there were
remains of a mosaic *(76)* of which the border survived with a band of pelta

(shield) motifs outside a band of guilloche (knot work). There was sufficient to establish a date on stylistic grounds of 325-50. Testimony to the use of braziers to heat the room was found in the scorch marks on the mosaic's surface.

North-east of the Ouse another mosaic dated to the early fourth century was found in excavations at 21-33 Aldwark (see also p.89) just outside the east corner of the fortress. As at Clementhorpe it was badly damaged, but clearly featured a woman's bust in a round panel, set centrally in a square area with a lozenge pattern. Because of the intrusion of the walls of the medieval church of St Helen little trace of the building which the mosaic had adorned survived, but presumably it had been another sizeable town house. The floor had been patched in places with coal and samian sherds, suggesting a long life.

While it appears that the civilian settlements of early fourth-century York contained a number of fine houses, it is not clear who lived in them. However, in view of, on the one hand, sparse evidence for manufacturing and long-distance trade at this time, and on the other, documentary evidence for the continuing importance of York as a military and administrative centre, it is possible that these houses were occupied by government officials or retired soldiers rather than by merchants or wealthy artisans.

The construction or reconstruction of fine houses in early fourth-century York may be seen alongside developments in the country villas in the region which indicate the continuing profitability of agriculture in at least certain parts of the city's hinterland. In fact the Clementhorpe house probably resembled a villa building and may have been at the centre of an estate little different in character from those estates in more distant areas. For example, at Beadlam near Helmsley in the Vale of Pickering, about 34km (20 miles) north of York, a new villa, albeit on the site of an earlier settlement, was built in the early fourth century. Although its remains are in a rather dilapidated condition, Beadlam is the only place north of the Humber where a villa building can be seen today. The main house had heated rooms and a mosaic floor, and it stood on the north side of a courtyard surrounded by other buildings not now visible. Further east on the Wolds the process of reconstruction and embellishment of a villa has been recorded at Rudston near Bridlington. In the residential block and bath suite mosaics were laid which are justly famous for their representations of Venus and Mercury. They bear witness to an interest in classical mythology even in this remote corner of the Roman world.

CHRISTIANITY IN ROMAN YORK

The iconography of the mosaics in the region's villas and in York itself shows that both prosperous town-dwellers and members of the landed gentry retained a consuming interest in religious matters. In the early fourth century a prominent topic of discussion was doubtless the merits of Christianity, the new faith which was spreading rapidly into the western empire. Christianity has many similarities with the mystery cults described above (pp.113-4) in having a theology which offered believers personal salvation and everlasting life. Christianity also offered adherents the idea of human equality before God and an injunction to love one's neighbour. The Christian message therefore had a unique and universal appeal to all sections of the community, rich and poor, men and women, Roman and barbarian, which other cults lacked. At the same time Christians suffered from persecution because they would not accept the other gods of the Roman world, in particular the divine emperor. Christianity proved strong enough to survive, of course, and it may have been a recognition of its growing popularity, rather than his legendary vision at the battle at the Milvian Bridge outside Rome in 312, which persuaded Constantine to accept the faith and turn its strength to his advantage.

Evidence for Christianity in Roman Britain comes largely from towns and villas. This may indicate that it was principally a religion of the upper echelons of society who travelled and came into contact with foreign influences, rather than one taken up by the rural masses who remained true to their local deities. There may also have been a regional aspect to the spread of Christianity, since the bulk of the artefacts and buildings which can be associated with the faith have come from south of the Humber, and there is, as yet, relatively little evidence from the north. Nonetheless, there was apparently a Christian community in Roman York since a bishop existed in 314 when 'Eborius the bishop for the city of York' was summoned by Constantine, along with three others from Britain, to discuss doctrinal matters at the Council of Arles. Archaeological traces of Christianity in York are, however, confined to just two artefacts. There is a tile from the Minster excavations on which is scratched the 'chi-rho', a monogram incorporating the first two letters of Christ's name in Greek. In addition a small bone plaque bearing a motto thought to be Christian in sentiment: SOROR AVE VIVAS IN DEO ('Hail sister may you live in God') was found with a burial in a stone coffin from Sycamore Terrace *(colour plate 14)*.

This burial raises the question of whether the spread of Christianity in Roman Britain can be detected in burial customs. The Christian emphasis on spiritual over material values which would seem to preclude grave goods may, it has been argued, explain the large number of unfurnished late Roman inhumation burials. In addition, the fact that in most late Roman cemeteries the bodies were usually aligned roughly east-west with their heads at the west end of the grave may also, it is suggested, be a Christian feature, as it would allow the dead to rise and face east at the sound of the last trump from the Holy Land. Unfortunately, the relationship between burial customs and religion is a complex one. East-west burial could be related to religious beliefs, but it may also indicate a purely practical concern to use the position of the sunrise to organise a cemetery in an orderly fashion. As regards the question of grave goods, the fact that the bone plaque with the supposed Christian motto was found in a burial with a glass jug, jewellery and other objects shows that one cannot regard the presence or absence of artefacts necessarily as an indication of a Christian or non-Christian interment.

The Christian belief in resurrection on the Day of Judgement has led some scholars to suggest that the distinctive late Roman practice of embalming the body of the deceased in gypsum (calcium sulphate), usually within a stone or lead coffin, may indicate a Christian burial. There are some 50 burials known from York in which the deceased was either completely or partially encased in gypsum. Of these, 17 are thought to be of certain fourth-century date. However, their find spots are not distributed so as to suggest a distinct area for Christian burial and it is probably correct to conclude that gypsum burial was simply a fashionable and expensive form of late Roman interment with no obvious religious associations.

LATE ROMAN CEMETERIES

It is difficult to determine in the current state of knowledge which parts of York's Roman cemeteries remained in use in the late Roman period. However, from the late third century onwards it seems that burials were often made on land closer to settled areas than had usually been the case hitherto. For example, burial at the Trentholme Drive site, at the south-western limit of the great cemetery which extended along the main approach road from the south-west, had ceased by about the year 280. North-east of the Ouse, at a site on Marygate, three late third-century inhumations were found only 200m (220 yards) north-west of the fortress. At 16-22 Coppergate, a small cemetery of six inhumation graves, probably of the mid- to late fourth century was found only 175m (190 yards) south-east of the legionary fortress close to where there had been stone buildings in the later third to early fourth century. The bodies had been buried in wooden coffins in graves on north-east/south-west or north-west/south-east alignments probably taken from the main axes of the fortress. In one case a group of iron hobnails indicated that the individual's boots had been buried with him; this is a custom known elsewhere and may symbolise the journey to the next world.

While explicit evidence for Christianity is, as already noted, difficult to identify in late Roman burials, there are signs in the cemeteries of fourth-century York of a change in attitude to the sanctity of earlier graves. At 35-41 Blossom Street the third-century mausoleum (p.122) had been deliberately dismantled by the early fourth century, when a cemetery was established containing some 25 graves aligned north-west/south-east, in other words at 90° to earlier interments (77). A number of graves were cut into the remains of the mausoleum and the burials within it. The fourth-century burials were in wooden coffins but without grave goods except in the case of an infant buried with two shale bracelets and a few glass beads (78).

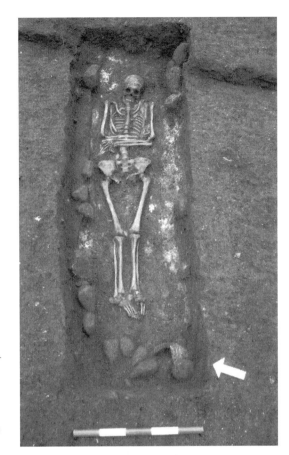

77 *(right)* 35–41 Blossom Street fourth-century burial: adult female in grave lined with stones (0.50m scale)

78 *(below)* 35–41 Blossom Street fourth-century burial: infant with shale bracelets

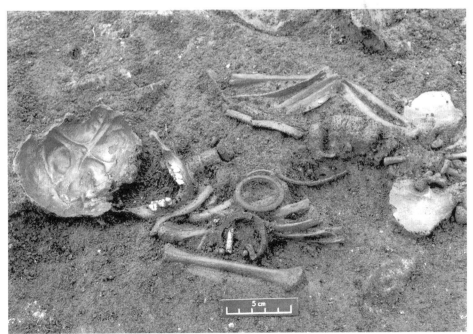

A break with previous traditions, involving abrupt changes in burial orientation and furnishing practice can also be found in other Romano-British cemeteries in the early fourth century and could indicate the spread of Christianity, but this cannot be proved at present.

There is also evidence from elsewhere for the destruction of temples and funerary monuments in the fourth century which could have been the work of Christians. This may be the context not only for the demolition of the mausoleum at Blossom Street, but also for the disturbance of prominent burials of earlier times at York. The sarcophagus of Aelia Severa (see p.118), for example, did not apparently contain her own body, but that of an adult male. The tombstone of a woman named Flavia Augustina had been re-used as its lid. The sarcophagi of Julia Fortunata and of another woman, Julia Victorina, also contained male skeletons.

ROMAN YORK AND THE END OF EMPIRE

The reign of Constantine and his sons was an era of strong government for the Roman empire and for a while invaders and rebels were successfully quelled. More troubled times returned to the west after the usurpation of Magnentius (350-3), another in a long line of army commanders who had ideas above his station. After defeating Magnentius, the emperor Constantius II (337-61) restored unified rule, but contemporary sources suggest that imperial security in the west suffered one disastrous blow after another in the second half of the fourth century. The historian Ammianus Marcellinus tells us that in 360 Britain was invaded by Picts and Scots leading to destruction in frontier areas, and that in 364 frontiers all over the empire, including Britain, were attacked. In 367 there was the so-called 'barbarian conspiracy', when by some unlucky chance there was an attack on Britain by Picts (from Scotland), Scots (from Ireland), and a tribe known as the Attacotti of unknown origin. They found the Roman army unequal to repelling them. A senior Roman officer was killed and the Dux, one Fullofaudes, was put out of action. In the aftermath the emperor Valentinian sent a high-ranking official, Count Theodosius, to restore Britain's defences.

Identifying building work which can be securely dated to the late 360s, and therefore Theodosius's work, is more or less impossible in Britain. However, as far as York is concerned, one can point to a certain amount of evidence for refurbishment in the fortress which is datable to the mid- to late fourth century. In the basilica of the headquarters building (*principia*), altars and statues of earlier times were removed and there was evidence, in the form of pedestal bases, for what were probably new statues in front of the nave columns. In front of one column there had been a railed enclosure, presumably around a statue or altar. Socketed bases sunk into the floor suggest that it had been

79 The archaeology of the mid-fourth century in the fortress: Minster Library site (1997) looking south-west showing: (foreground) a pebble surface and post-holes thought to have supported a veranda on south-east side of a building, (centre) a stone-lined drain, probably an eaves-drip for the veranda, and (top) a further pebble surface (2m scale)

possible to screen-off the north-western bays of the nave and aisles, but for what purpose is uncertain. Built out into the portico space at the north-west end of the basilica was an additional room which was decorated with a very fine scheme of painted wall plaster (now displayed in the Minster Undercroft, see p.66; *colour plate 15*). The function of this room is unknown, but it may have provided private accommodation for a senior officer, perhaps the *Dux Britanniarum* himself.

Elsewhere in the fortress, observations of sewer trench repairs in Low Petergate in 1998 revealed that the gravel surface of the *via principalis* noted above (p.36) was overlain by a deposit of dark silt up to 20mm (8in) thick, which contained a sherd of pottery datable to about the year 350 or later. This deposit was succeeded by a rather rough and ready street surface composed largely of re-used building materials suggesting demolition of structures in the vicinity. In addition, a re-metalling of the *intervallum* street was recorded in a trench at the Bedern (near the east corner; Site 8 on *13*), again after the accumulation of a layer of silt on the late second-century surface. At the Minster Library the latest street recorded was also mid-fourth century and there was evidence for refurbishment of buildings, in one instance apparently with a veranda, a traditional Roman feature still deemed appropriate for military accommodation *(79)*. At Interval Towers SW5 and SW6 the latest re-cutting of the fortress ditch may also belong to the second half of the fourth century.

80 The 'Anglian Tower' (foreground), probably fourth-century, set into the fortress wall as seen from the north-east. The Multangular Tower is at the top right. The stone wall on the left belonged to the medieval hospital of St Leonard and the wall on the extreme right is the medieval city wall. The ramparts of Roman and later date have been recreated bottom left

An addition to the fortress defences which may belong to this period is the so-called Anglian Tower *(80)*. This is a rectangular stone structure, standing about 60m (200ft) north-east of the Multangular Tower. It was originally discovered in 1842 and re-excavated in 1970. The tower now stands about 4m (13ft) high and measures about 4.5m (14ft 6in) square. It is built of roughly coursed and dressed oolitic limestone, in contrast to the vast majority of the fortress buildings, which are of magnesian limestone. The tower has opposing doorways with simple arches; the original roof was replaced with a brick barrel vault in the nineteenth century. The tower wall footings are shallow, but the front of the structure was founded on the base of a cut into the fortress wall and the rear stands on the rampart, which was reduced in height at this point.

The 1970 excavation was not able to offer any conclusive evidence for the date of the tower, although it was obviously later than the fortress wall and earlier than a bank strengthened with rough stonework which had been built on top of the Roman rampart. This bank is thought to have been a replacement of the fortress wall's derelict parapet and it contained one or two sherds of Anglian (eighth- to ninth-century) pottery. One reason for suggesting a post-Roman date for the tower appears to be the notion that the cut into the fortress wall was an enhancement of a gap already created by dilapidation. This must have taken place, so the argument continues, after the Roman army had departed, since it would surely have repaired the wall had it been in residence. Even if this dilapidation had happened, there is no reason for a tower rather than a stretch of walling to be used to plug a gap. It might equally well be asked, of course, why a new tower was needed in Roman times, since there was already a perfectly good one, NW1, nearby. The answer may be that Interval Tower NW1 had become unsafe. In the 1971 excavation to expose the fortress wall the tower walls were found to have parted from it, probably due to subsidence, the effects of which have been observed in several other places around the fortress wall circuit. If NW1 had subsided in the Roman period this would provide a simple explanation for a replacement nearby.

Another argument for giving the Anglian Tower a late-Roman date has been developed by Dr Paul Buckland of Sheffield University and rests on his analysis of the building stone. Jurassic oolite was, as noted above (pp.53-4), extensively used in Roman York, but there is no evidence for its further use until medieval times. No newly built Anglian stone buildings are known in the city and the stone used in the Anglo-Scandinavian period, particularly for churches, was largely, if not exclusively, salvaged from redundant Roman buildings. The fact that the Anglian tower contains no re-used stone implies, Buckland suggests, that the Roman fortress buildings were still in use and, therefore, he concludes the tower must be Roman.

As far as the Roman forts of the Yorkshire region are concerned, some, such as Bainbridge in Wensleydale and Ilkley in Wharfedale, which both controlled key Pennine passes, underwent reconstruction in the second half of the fourth century. An addition to the region's defences, however, was a series of five so-called 'signal stations' on the Yorkshire coast at (from north to south) Huntcliff (near Saltburn), Goldsborough, Ravenscar, Scarborough and Filey *(81)*. The first named is some 70km (40 miles) north of York and the last named 60km (36 miles) to the north-east. Dating of the signal stations is uncertain, but they are probably later than 367. Invaders in this and other years may have avoided the Hadrian's Wall frontier by sailing along the unprotected coastline. The signal stations were probably intended to provide warning and protection for local people in the event of any attack. The sites measured about 50m (164ft) across and were essentially towers within a small walled courtyard defended by a bank and ditch - '*turrum et castrum*' as described on an inscription, the latest from Roman Britain, found at the presumed signal station site at Ravenscar. The height of the towers is unknown, but as much as 20m (66ft) is possible. At times of danger beacons mounted on the towers may have been used to co-ordinate Roman naval patrols and contact the fort at Malton where a unit known, appropriately perhaps, as the *Numerus Supervenientium Petuariensium* - 'the anticipators' of *Petuaria* (Brough-on- Humber) – is known to have been stationed . If matters were really serious then presumably the army at York could be called out.

81 Reconstruction (looking south-east) of the late fourth-century Roman signal station on the Carr Naze, Filey, North Yorkshire

The imperial authorities must have hoped that Theodosius had secured Britain for the forseeable future, but if so they were over-optimistic. Both archaeological and written evidence show that in the last two or three decades of the fourth century the beginnings of radical change in the established order were taking place. One reason for this was probably a gradual diminution in the size of the Roman forces in Britain as a succession of usurpers, of whom Magnus Maximus in 383 was but the first, removed troops from York and elsewhere to challenge for the imperial crown. By about the year 410, the date frequently given for the end of Britain's inclusion in the Roman empire, there can have been few soldiers at *Eboracum* worthy to be considered heirs to the proud tradition of Petilius Cerialis and his men of 71.

By way of a footnote to this discussion of late fourth-century defence matters, we may note a representation of what may be a Roman soldier on a late fourth-century fragment of Crambeck ware pottery from York *(colour plate 16)*. He appears to brandish a weapon in his right hand, but the object resembling a frying pan in his left is not easy to identify. If this is not a soldier then, in view of the shape of the figure, which corresponds to that of the constellation of Orion, another possible identification of him is as the handsome giant and huntsman beloved of the goddess Diana.

Archaeological evidence for the last years of the Roman era in York is sparse and the subject requires a great deal of further research. One obstacle to this is the extent of disturbance of late Roman deposits and structures by later pits and cellars. Another is that determining whether layers at the end of the Roman sequence which have been excavated belong to the last decades of the fourth or to the early fifth century is very difficult. They often contain large quantities of artefacts which are thought to be fourth-century because they cannot usually be associated with coins minted later than the year 402, by which time the supply to Britain had all but ceased. It is likely, however, that coins circulated for a while after 402 before finding their way into the ground. Furthermore, it seems probable that pottery in Roman style was still made in, perhaps, the first quarter of the fifth century, but the wares cannot as yet be positively identified.

In the fortress it would appear that from about the year 380 onwards the character of occupation in the headquarters basilica, the first cohort barracks and the buildings at 9 Blake Street changed markedly. At 9 Blake Street the principal building range (see pp.76-8) had been largely demolished before the end of the fourth century *(82)*. The kitchen range, however, appears to have remained standing throughout the century and layers within it, containing

82 The archaeology of the late fourth century in the fortress: 9 Blake Street. Features and surfaces cut by medieval intrusions (looking north-east – see Illustration *40* for plan of mid-second-century arrangement). All the walls were demolished in the late- or post-Roman periods, but in the foreground are the remains of the rear wall of the barracks. A 2m scale rests on deposits covering the latest surface of the cobbled street. Behind lies the kitchen range of the buildings with two stone surfaces – floors – immediately to the left of the dividing wall. At the top of the picture beyond the passage way (with a second 2m scale resting on it) is the main room of the residential block at an earlier level

coins dated after 388, were overlain by mortar floors and further layers containing domestic refuse (largely bones and pottery). The street on the south-west side of the site and the passages between the buildings were resurfaced from time to time. It is not entirely clear what is signified by the changes in layout and standards of maintenance revealed here, but by the end of the fourth century the remaining garrison were apparently not observing the discipline of former years and may have lived with their families and other civilians in the fortress. Some support for this theory comes from the headquarters' basilica in the form of an episode which may belong to the last years of the fourth century or to the early years of the fifth. At the south-east end of the building the rear range behind (i.e. to the north-east of) the north-east aisle produced evidence for a workshop with metalworking hearths. Hearths were also found in the centurion's quarters of the first cohort barracks. At both the north-west and south-east end of the basilica the floors composed of crushed tile were overlain by an accumulation of deposits containing copious animal bone originating perhaps in a nearby butchery.

In the civilian settlements the mid-fourth century is marked by a divergence in fortunes between, on the one hand, the *colonia* south-west of the Ouse (assumed to be defended) and, on the other, settled areas both south-west of the Ouse outside the defences and north-east of the river outside the fortress. In the *colonia*, settlement clearly continued until the end of the Roman period, whilst in the other areas no site has produced good evidence for occupation except for the house at Clementhorpe.

Within the *colonia* we must return to the Wellington Row site *(83)*, where a remarkable sequence of deposits and structural remains was, unusually, preserved undisturbed by later intrusions. It probably extended from the late fourth century into the early fifth, although further research on the finds will be needed to confirm this. What has been identified as the latest floor surface in the stone building described above (pp.94-7) was very rough, being composed of cobbles and beaten earth. It probably dates to about the year 360. It was on this surface that a dark silty deposit began to accumulate containing, in the first instance, large quantities of pottery and animal bones, presumably the product of refuse disposal. The deposit also contained some seven hundred small bronze coins, the almost valueless small change of the fourth century which was minted in huge quantities during episodes of inflation. More unusual items included a number of bone combs *(84)* and a fragment of jet plaque bearing the image of a male figure in relief *(85)*.

In due course the dark silty deposit built up within the building to a depth of about 0.8m (2ft 6in) in places. Comparable material, often known as 'dark earth', overlying the latest identifiable Roman structures and pre-dating those of late Anglo-Saxon and Anglo-Scandinavian or medieval date is a common phenomenon on urban sites in Britain. The forces creating the dark earth are varied, but analysis suggests that a substantial component was probably decay-

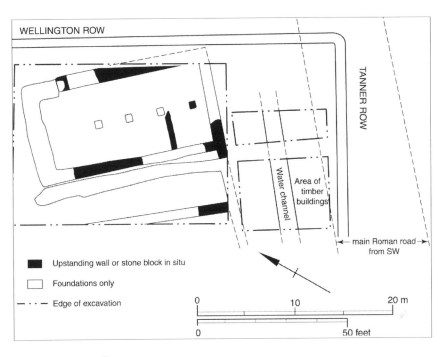

WELLINGTON ROW

TANNER ROW

Water channel

Area of
timber
buildings

← main Roman road →
from SW

■ Upstanding wall or stone block in situ

□ Foundations only

— · · — Edge of excavation

0   10   20 m

0   50 feet

Clockwise from top:

83 Wellington Row: plan of late fourth-century features

84 Wellington Row: a group of bone combs from late fourth-century 'dark earth' deposits

85 Wellington Row: figure in relief on an incomplete jet plaque found in a fourth-century layer (height 45mm)

ing plant material, dead leaves and the like, mixed with domestic and other refuse indicated both in York and elsewhere by a large quantity of artefacts. This need not mean, however, that late-Roman towns were densely populated. Instead 'dark earth' may indicate a changed approach to refuse disposal involving a lowering of standards and a change of use for areas previously in occupation. It was obviously easier to get rid of rubbish by throwing it into a disused building near one's home than it was to carry it some distance to an extramural dump. By about the year 400 the Wellington Row building had probably become derelict as wind and rain eroded away the mortar between the stones in the exposed parts of the walls of what had become essentially a large rectangular rubbish pit.

In dark earth deposits found in trenches excavated across the centre of the Wellington Row site the artefacts were finely broken up, suggesting a reworking of the material by agriculture, datable by a small number of pot sherds and other artefacts to the Anglian period (eighth-ninth century). Within the stone building, however, pottery and bone often occurred in large pieces and had clearly not been disturbed after deposition. The reason for this is probably that a timber building, to some extent re-using its walls as footings, had been erected within the stone structure. At the time the first edition of this book was written it was thought that this timber building was late Roman, but it now seems more likely to belong to the Anglian period.

At some stage in the fourth century the great main road from the south-west appears to have been narrowed to perhaps half its width and its history in the late fourth and fifth centuries could not be determined as the carriage-way now lay beyond (i.e. south-east of) the Wellington Row site under the modern street Tanner Row. Within the site timber structures were found to have been erected on the disused part of the surface. Little can be said about them as the remains only survived modern cellars in a very restricted area, but a number of post bases packed around with cobbles were found along with a sequence of pebble and mortar floors. It is possible that these structures were stalls set up by the road side to provide refreshments or other commodities for travellers crossing the river. Behind (i.e. north-west of) the building remains, and probably contemporary with them, a most remarkable trench was found. It was some 2m (6ft 6in) wide and 1m (3ft 3in) deep, and had been cut into the road, following its alignment. The trench sides were more or less vertical and the base was flat; cut into the sides and base was a series of slots and post-holes in which iron nails survived. These features must indicate that the trench had a wooden lining and this was probably intended to aid retention of water. The trench was, therefore, probably a simple version of the stone-lined channel with the lead pipes which was laid down in the mid-second century (pp.93-4) and there was evidence that pits had been dug to remove these pipes at much the same time as the wood-lined trench was installed.

A summary of evidence from other sites for the end of the civilian settlements may begin at 1–9 Micklegate. The hypocaust openings in the great bath building were blocked at some stage in the second half of the fourth century *(63)* and the original floor was demolished, leading to the creation of a room with a floor sunk below contemporary ground level. Subsequently, the walls of the building were demolished to more or less the height at which they were found in the excavation and the room was filled with rubble. This probably took place towards the end of the Roman period, and the next phase of activity was in the seventh to eighth century (see p.151). Demolition must have involved a very substantial effort and one wonders why it was done.

In the house excavated at St Mary Bishophill Senior the hypocaust is thought to have become obsolete before the end of the fourth century, although occupation may have continued. In the house at St Mary Bishophill Junior it is apparent that there was a change in the character of occupation towards the end of the fourth century, when the drains were reorganised in a rather rough-and-ready manner, and a dump of refuse containing copious herring bones was made. Late-Roman refuse dumping in the form of dark earth has been identified at other sites including General Accident, 5 Rougier Street and 37-8 Bishophill Senior, but the deposits in each case had been heavily disturbed in the medieval period by rubbish pits and trenches dug to recover stone from the Roman walls.

The impression has sometimes been created in popular historical literature that the sort of changes in the urban order outlined above were symptomatic of Britain collapsing into anarchy at the end of the Roman period. However, there is no reason why this should be the picture which immediately comes to mind when considering York in the late fourth and early fifth centuries. Rather, we should think in terms of a society reordering its priorities to cope with a situation in which an economy heavily reliant on serving the military and the provincial government was proving impossible to sustain. There was, of course, a lowering of standards of building and road maintenance, and a decline in population numbers, but the end of Roman York arrived – to paraphrase T.S. Eliot – not with a disorderly bang as the barbarians rushed in but with a dignified whimper as the imperial regime simply ceased to function.

POSTSCRIPT – A CITY REBORN

Although good archaeological evidence for much of the fifth and sixth centuries is virtually non-existent, it cannot be assumed that what had been Roman York was either entirely deserted or lacking a role in the economy and society of its region. In a period when imperial power had probably devolved to competing local leaders, the importance of York as both a defendable stronghold and crucial river crossing is unlikely to have been overlooked. It can be envisaged, furthermore, that the local population remained aware of Roman York's former role as a centre of political and religious authority. For anyone tempted to revive such authority the city also possessed the appropriate, if perhaps somewhat run-down, amenities for any associated functions and ceremonies.

By the late fifth century York may have found itself, firstly, at the eastern limit of a British kingdom known as *Elmet*, which is thought to have occupied much of Yorkshire to the west of the city, and, secondly, on the western edge of territory controlled by incoming Anglian people from what are now north Germany and Denmark. Evidence for an Anglian population in the York area itself at this time takes the form of two cemeteries, one at Heworth and the other on The Mount, in which pagan burials in cremation urns were found. Both cemeteries lay within former Roman cemeteries, suggesting perhaps some continuity of sacred associations. They were also sited close to main Roman roads which may have remained in use. In the early seventh century *Elmet* was conquered by the Anglian King Edwin of Northumbria. Edwin was to return York to the mainstream of history in the year 627 when, according to the Venerable Bede, he had himself baptised here in a small wooden church. The location of this church is unknown, but it was probably near the present Minster in the centre of the former Roman fortress.

The survival of the line of Roman roads around York and of Roman streets in the city itself into the medieval and modern periods may indicate their continuing use in the most obscure years of the post-Roman period, but this is difficult to demonstrate archaeologically. As far as the fortress is concerned, Petergate, Stonegate and Chapter House Street run close to the lines of the principal Roman thoroughfares. However, the observations in Low Petergate, referred to above (p.141), demonstrated that there was no continuity of use between the Roman *via principalis* and the earliest medieval street of the eleventh century. The late-Roman street was buried under over 1m (3ft 3in) of dark silt. The only continuity of use from Roman to medieval probably took place at the fortress gates, the location of which has clearly been a principal determinant of the lines of the medieval streets. However, when the line of Petergate, which more or less follows the *via principalis* between the sites of the former Roman gates at Bootham Bar and King's Square, is plotted on a plan of the fortress *(13)* it can be seen to have run through only the south-western portals of those gates, suggesting that the other portal had been blocked. Blocking of gates or gate portals is a well-known phenomenon in Roman forts in the fourth century on Hadrian's Wall and elsewhere, but the date of any blocking at York is unknown and could be post-Roman. In due course the Roman gates were demolished, but the line of Petergate was by then fixed.

On the south-west bank of the Ouse the enclosure thought to have been created by the Roman defences was probably re-fortified at the time of the Norman Conquest and the main Roman gate was, it is suggested, replaced by Micklegate Bar. How long the Roman river crossing survived is, however, unknown and so is the fate of the great main road leading to it. Only two short stretches of medieval and now modern street overlie the Roman line, one near the Bar and the other, part of Tanner Row, near the crossing itself. The road line may, however, have survived into the later part of the Anglian period, and the survival of other elements in the Roman townscape is suggested by the north-east/south-west alignment of two early churches, St Mary Bishophill Senior (now demolished) and St Mary Bishophill Junior. The mid-eleventh-century tower of the latter is built entirely of stone from a Roman building which must have survived in some form until about the time of the Norman Conquest.

At 1-9 Micklegate (p.149) there was intriguing evidence for re-use of the remains of a Roman building in the Anglian period. Although the walls of the baths had probably been demolished in the late fourth century, their location was apparently still known, as post-holes of a timber structure were found neatly cut into the top of two of them. Associated with this building were three human inhumation burials. Although one of them was accompanied by two knives, they were probably Christians, which may mean the post-hole building was a church, perhaps the forerunner of nearby St John's Micklegate.

The Vikings seized York in 876, and some time thereafter a major alteration was made to the city's layout, which finally rendered the line of the Roman road from the south-west within the *colonia* enclosure redundant. The street Micklegate was created which curves away from what had probably been the Roman gate at or near Micklegate Bar to Ouse Bridge 250m (270 yards) downstream from the Roman crossing. On the north-east bank of the Ouse the new street continued to the north-east as Ousegate and Pavement. It was also during the Anglo-Scandinavian period (876-1066) that most Roman buildings still surviving in York, including the great fortress basilica (6), were largely demolished. Roman York became in effect a great quarry, principally for church-builders both in the city itself and in its region. Only parts of the fortress defences and perhaps the Roman defences south-west of the Ouse survived the onslaught. By the Norman Conquest *Eboracum* was much less of a physical presence than it had been 200 years earlier, but nonetheless it remained a powerful influence on the minds of citizens. For example, as late as the sixteenth century some early maps of England still used the Roman name to refer to York.

We have now come full circle back to the time of the earliest antiquaries of Tudor and Stuart times referred to in Chapter 1, whose imagination was captured by the possibility of rediscovering the physical remains of the 'gran-

86 Brooches made in a modern idiom, based on Roman originals by jewellers Charmian Ottaway and Peter Moulton for the Yorkshire Museum

deur that was Rome' on the banks of the Ouse. The descendants of those pioneering scholars are now literally 'legion' in their numbers and include men and women of all sorts and conditions, not only archaeologists but students, artists, craftspeople *(86)*, re-enactment enthusiasts, tourists from all parts of the globe, and last but not least, local residents. It is in anticipation of many great discoveries to come that I offer this book on Roman York to you all.

FURTHER READING

A good starting point for further reading about Roman York is *Eburacum*, Volume 1 of the inventory of York by the Royal Commission on Historical Monuments for England, published in 1962. The reader may also find some interest and amusement in earlier works, including Francis Drake's *Eboracum* (published in 1736), William Hargrove's *History of York* (1818), and Charles Wellbeloved's *Eburacum* (1842).

Since 1962, aspects of Roman York have been discussed in *Soldier and Civilian in Roman Yorkshire* edited by R.M. Butler and published in 1971 by Leicester University Press. It includes the following papers which relate specifically to Roman York: B.R. Hartley, 'Roman York and the northern military command to the third century AD', pp.55-70; E.B. Birley, 'The fate of the ninth legion', pp.71-80; R.M. Butler, 'The defences of the fourth-century fortress at York', pp.97-106 (now largely superseded by recent research); B.M. Dickinson and K.F. Hartley, 'The evidence of potters' stamps on samian ware and on mortaria for the trading connections of Roman York', pp.127-42; A.F. Norman, 'Religion in Roman York', pp.143-54.

In 1984, papers on the archaeology of York appeared in *Archaeological Papers from York presented to M.W. Barley* edited by P.V. Addyman and V.E. Black, published by York Archaeological Trust. The following are still relevant for the Roman period: P.V. Addyman, 'York in its archaeological setting', pp.7-21; R.F.J. Jones, 'The cemeteries of Roman York', pp.34-42; A.B. Sumpter, 'Interval towers and the spaces between', pp.46-50; P.C. Buckland, 'The Anglian Tower and the use of Jurassic limestone in York', pp.51-7.

Detailed publication of excavations in York since 1972 is to be found in the fascicules of the *Archaeology of York* series, published for York Archaeological Trust by the Council for British Archaeology under the general editorship of Peter Addyman. The following concern the Roman period:

Volume 3, *The Legionary Fortress*
1. J.B. Whitwell, 1976. *The Church Street Sewer and an Additional Building*
2. A.B. Sumpter and S. Coll, 1977. *Interval Tower SW5 and the South-west defences: Excavations 1972-75*
3. P. Ottaway, 1993. *Excavations and Observations on and adjacent to the Defences 1971-90*
4. R.A. Hall, 1997. *Excavations in the* Praetentura: *9 Blake Street*

Volume 4, *The Colonia*
1. M.O.H. Carver, S. Donaghey and A.B. Sumpter, 1978. *Riverside Structures and a Well in Skeldergate and Buildings in Bishophill*

Volume 6, *Roman Extra-mural Settlement and Roads*
1. D.A. Brinklow, R.A. Hall, J.R. Magilton and S. Donaghey, 1986. *Coney Street, Aldwark and Clementhorpe, Minor Sites and Roads*
2. P. Ottaway, in prep. *Excavations on Blossom Street, at 16-22 Coppergate and other Sites*

Volume 14, *The Past Environment of York*
1. P. Buckland, 1976. *The Environmental Evidence from the Church Street Roman Sewer*
2. H.K. Kenward and D. Williams, 1979. *Biological Evidence from the Roman Warehouses in Coney Street*
3. A.R. Hall, H.K. Kenward and D. Williams, 1980. *Environmental Evidence from Roman Deposits in Skeldergate*
5. H.K. Kenward, A.R. Hall and A.K.G. Jones, 1986. *Environmental Evidence from a Roman Well and Anglian Pits in the Legionary Fortress*
6. A.R. Hall and H.K. Kenward, 1990. *Environmental Evidence from the* Colonia: *General Accident and Rougier Street*

Roman York

Volume 15, *The Animal Bones*
2. T.P. O'Connor, 1988. *Bones from the General Accident Site*

Volume 16, *The Pottery*
2. J.R. Perrin, 1981. *Roman pottery from the* Colonia: *Skeldergate and Bishophill*
4. J.R. Perrin, 1990. *Roman Pottery from the* Colonia 2: *General Accident and Rougier Street*
7. J. Monaghan, 1993. *Roman Pottery from the Fortress*
8. J. Monaghan, 1997. *Roman Pottery from York*

Volume 17, *The Small Finds*
1. A. MacGregor, 1978. *Roman Finds from Skeldergate and Bishophill*
10. H.E.M. Cool, G. Lloyd-Morgan and A.D. Hooley, 1995. *Finds from the Fortress*

Regular accounts of current excavations appear in *Yorkshire Archaeology Today*, published twice a year by York Archaeological Trust. Summary annual reports on excavations in York and its region appear in *Britannia*, the journal of the Roman Society.

Other specialist publications on Roman York and related topics may be found under the following headings:

The fortress and the Roman army in York
Dyer, J. and Wenham, P., 1967. 'Excavations and discoveries in a cellar in Messrs Chas Hart's premises, Feasegate, York, 1956', *Yorkshire Archaeological Journal* 39, 419-25
Miller, S., 1925. 'Roman York: Excavations of 1925', *Journal of Roman Studies* 15, 176-94
Miller, S., 1928. 'Roman York: Excavations of 1926-1927', *Journal of Roman Studies* 18, 61-99
Phillips, D. and Heywood, B., 1995. *Excavations at York Minster, volume 1: From Roman Fortress to Norman Cathedral* (HMSO, London)
Radley, J., 1966. 'A section of the Roman fortress wall at Barclay's Bank, St Helen's Square, York', *Yorkshire Archaeological Journal* 41, 581-4
Radley, J., 1970. 'Two interval towers and new sections of the fortress wall, York', *Yorkshire Archaeological Journal* 42, 399-402
Radley, J., 1972. 'Excavations in the defences of the City of York: an early medieval stone tower and the successive earth ramparts', *Yorkshire Archaeological Journal* 44, 38-64
Ramm, H.G., 1956. 'Roman York: excavations of 1955', *Journal of Roman Studies* 46, 76-90
Stead, I.M., 1958. 'Excavations at the south corner tower of the Roman fortress at York 1956', *Yorkshire Archaeological Journal* 39, 515-8
Stead, I.M., 1968. 'An excavation at King's Square, York, 1957', *Yorkshire Archaeological Journal* 42, 151-64
Wenham, L.P., 1961. 'Excavations and discoveries adjoining the south-west wall of the Roman legionary fortress in Feasegate, York, 1955-57', *Yorkshire Archaeological Journal* 40, 329-50
Wenham, L.P., 1962. 'Excavations and discoveries within the legionary fortress in Davygate, York, 1955-8', *Yorkshire Archaeological Journal* 40, 507-87
Wenham, L.P., 1968. 'Discoveries in King's Square, York, 1963', *Yorkshire Archaeological Journal* 42, 165-8
Wenham, L.P., 1972. 'Excavations in Low Petergate, York, 1957-8', *Yorkshire Archaeological Journal* 44, 65-113

The Civilian Settlements and Cemeteries
King, E., 1975. 'Roman kiln material from the Borthwick Institute, Peasholme Green: a report for the York Excavation Group', in P.V. Addyman, Excavations in York 1972-3, First Interim Report. *Antiquaries Journal* 54, 213-7
Ottaway, P., 1999. 'York: the study of a late Roman *colonia*', in H. Hurst (ed.), *The Coloniae of Roman Britain: New Studies and a Review*, Journal of Roman Archaeology Supplementary Series 36, 136-51
Ramm, H.G., 1976. 'The Church of St Mary Bishophill Senior, York: Excavation 1964', *Yorkshire Archaeological Journal* 48, 35-68
Wenham, L.P., 1965. 'Blossom Street excavations, 1953-5', *Yorkshire Archaeological Journal* 41, 524-90
Wenham, L.P., 1968. *The Romano-British Cemetery at Trentholme Drive, York*, Ministry of Public Buildings and Works Archaeological Report 5

154

Artefacts and Inscriptions

Allason-Jones, L., 1996. *Roman Jet in the Yorkshire Museum* (York, Yorkshire Museum)

Birley, E., 1966. 'The Roman inscriptions of York', *Yorkshire Archaeological Journal* 41, 726–34

Cool, H.E.M., 1998. 'Early occupation at St Mary's Abbey, York: the evidence of the glass', in J. Bird (ed.), *Form and Fabric: Studies in Rome's Material Past in Honour of B.R. Hartley*, Oxbow Monograph 80, 301–5

Collingwood, R.G. and Wright, R.P., 1965. *Roman Inscriptions of Britain* (Oxford)

Cool, H.E.M., 2002. 'Craft and industry in Roman York', in P. Wilson and J. Price (eds), *Aspects of Industry in Roman York and the North* (Oxford), 1–11

Cool, H.E.M., Jackson, C.M. and Monaghan. J., 1999. 'Glass-making and the Sixth Legion at York', *Britannia* 30, 147–62

Swan, V.G., 1992. 'Legio VI and its men: African legionaries in Britain', *Journal of Roman Pottery Studies* 5, 1–33

Swan, V.G. and McBride, R.M., 2002. 'A Rhineland potter at the legionary fortress of York', in M. Aldhouse-Green and P. Webster, *Artefacts and Archaeology. Aspects of the Celtic and Roman World* (Cardiff), 190–234

Wright, R.P., 1976. 'Tile stamps of the sixth legion found in Britain', *Britannia* 7, 224–235

Wright, R.P., 1978. 'Tile stamps of the ninth legion found in Britain', *Britannia* 9, 379–82

For readers with an interest in the people of Roman Britain, including York, and in Roman inscriptions, an excellent introduction is to be found in A.R. Birley, *The People of Roman Britain* (1979). The same author has written *Septimius Severus: The African Emperor* (1988), which in Chapter 16 covers the visit to York.

Roman Yorkshire

The literature on Roman Yorkshire is extensive, but for a summary account readers are referred to a paper by the present author published in 2003 and entitled 'The Roman period in the Yorkshire region: a rapid resource assessment', in T.G. Manby, S. Moorhouse and P. Ottaway (eds), *The Archaeology of Yorkshire: An Assessment at the Beginning of the 21st Century*, Yorkshire Archaeological Society Occasional Paper 3, pp.125–49. In addition, there are useful papers in the British Archaeological Reports, British Series Volume 193 edited by J. Price and P.R. Wilson entitled *Recent Research in Roman Yorkshire* (1988). Papers of particular relevance for York itself include: B. Hartley, 'Plus ça change…', or reflections on the Roman forts of Yorkshire', pp.153–60; R.F.J. Jones 'The hinterland of Roman York', pp.161–70 and P.C. Buckland. 'The stones of York: building materials in Roman Yorkshire', pp.237–87.

Another useful paper concerned with York and its region is by S. Roskams: 'The hinterlands of Roman York: present patterns and future strategies', in H. Hurst (ed.), *The Coloniae of Roman Britain: New Studies and a Review*, Journal of Roman Archaeology Supplementary Series 36, 45–72.

In addition, there are two volumes in the *Peoples of Roman Britain* series: H.G. Ramm, *The Parisi* (1978); B.R. Hartley and L. Fitts, *The Brigantes* (1988).

The villas at Beadlam, Dalton Parlours and Rudston were published as follows:

Neal, D.S., 1996. *Excavations on the Roman Villa at Beadlam, Yorkshire*, Yorkshire Archaeological Report 2

Stead, I.M., 1980. *Rudston Roman Villa* (Leeds, Yorkshire Archaeological Society)

Wrathmell, S., and Nicholson, A., 1990. *Dalton Parlours, Iron Age Settlement and Roman Villa*, Yorkshire Archaeology 3

The Filey Roman signal station and a review of the stations as a group appears in:

Ottaway, P., 2000. 'Excavations on the site of the Roman signal station at Carr Naze, Filey, 1993-94', *Archaeological Journal* 157, 79–199

Reviews of the evidence for craft and industry appears in P. Wilson and J. Price (eds), *Aspects of Industry in Roman York and the North* (Oxford).

GLOSSARY

Latin terms used for principal parts of the Roman fortress at York are as follows:

Intervallum – the space around the perimeter between the fortress buildings and the rampart.

Latera praetorii – the areas on either side of the headquarters building (*principia*).

Porta decumana – the main fortress gate at the end of the *via decumana*, at York the north-east gate.

Porta praetorian – the main fortress gate at the end of the *via praetoria*, at York the south-west gate.

Porta principalis dextra and *porta principalis sinistra* – the main fortress gates at each end of the *via principalis*, at York the former is the north-west gate and the latter the south-east.

Praetentura – that part of the fortress lying in front of the *principia*, at York on its south-west side.

Praetorium – the commanding officer's house.

Principia – the fortress headquarters building.

Retentura – that part of the fortress lying behind the *principia*, at York on its north-east side.

Via decumana – the main street running from the rear of the *principia* to the *porta decumana*.

Via praetoria – the main street running from the front of the *principia* to the main gate, the *porta praetoria*.

Via principalis – the main street running across the fortress in front of the *principia*, at York it is aligned north-west/south-east.

Via quintana – a main street running across the fortress behind the *principia*, at York it is aligned north-west/south-east.

Via sagularis – the street running around the fortress defences in the *intervallum* space.

OTHER LATIN TERMS

Aedes – shrine.

Colonia (plural *coloniae*) – literally colony, but the term also refers to the highest grade of Roman town, one populated largely by Roman citizens.

Genius – spirit used in the phrase '*genius loci*', meaning the 'spirit of the place'.

Numen – divine power, a term used in connection with worship of the emperor, dedications were made to the imperial *numen*.

Opus signinum – a form of Roman concrete which includes fragments of tile to improve water resistant qualities.

Pes monetalis (pM) – the Roman foot, a unit of measurement widely used in the Roman fortress at York, equivalent to about 0.296m or 0.97 imperial feet. *Monetalis* refers to the standard held in the temple of Juno Moneta in Rome.

Triclinium (plural *triclinia*) – the dining room in a Roman house.

SITES TO VISIT

The Yorkshire Museum

The museum is in Museum Gardens and houses a fine collection of Roman antiquities. There are sculptures, tombstones, mosaics and numerous artefacts from York, many of them from the cemeteries. Also on display are Iron Age artefacts from Stanwick, and Roman finds from excavations at Catterick, Dalton Parlours and other sites in Yorkshire. Open daily. For information see www.yorkshiremuseum.org.uk

YORK: THE ROMAN FORTRESS

The East Corner. This can be seen along with Interval Tower NE6 from the medieval walls. Ascend at Monk Bar in Goodramgate or at Layerthorpe Postern on the corner of Jewbury and Peasholme Green. The precinct in which the remains stand is usually kept locked, although access can be arranged by permission of the City of York Council.

The Multangular Tower and Anglian Tower. They can be seen in the Museum Gardens along with fine stretches of the fortress wall. Access during daylight hours.

The Principia. Remains of the headquarters basilica and finds from the Minster excavations can be seen in the Minster Undercroft. Access in the Minster south transept. Open daily. For information see www.yorkminster.org

The baths *caldarium.* Part of the *caldarium* of the legionary baths, originally excavated in 1930-1, can be seen in the Roman Bath public house. For opening hours contact the landlord.

ROMAN YORKSHIRE

Sites referred to in this book include:

Aldborough Roman town (*Isurium Brigantum*). The site is 27km (17 miles) north-west of York, near Boroughbridge. A stretch of the town defences and two in situ mosaics are visible and there is a small site museum. In the care of English Heritage, for more details see www.english-heritage.org.uk

Beadlam villa. The site lies on the road between Helmsley and Pickering opposite the turning to Pockley. Access by permission of the landowner.

Malton (*Derventio*) Fort and Museum. Malton is 27km (17 miles) north-east of York. The fort rampart can be seen in Orchard Field on the east side of the road to Pickering about 500m north of the town centre. The museum is in the Market Place and houses a good collection of finds from Malton itself and from the villas of east Yorkshire. For opening hours Tel: 01653 695136.

Scarborough Roman Signal Station. The remains are in the grounds of Scarborough Castle. The site is in the care of English Heritage.

Kingston-upon-Hull. The museum is in the High Street and amongst a large collection of Roman material there are the mosaics from Rudston villa. For more details and opening times, visit www.hullcc.gov.uk/museums.

INDEX

Page numbers with illustrations are given in **bold**

If you are interested in purchasing
other books published by The History Press, or in case you have
difficulty finding any of our books in your local bookshop,
you can also place orders directly through our website

www.thehistorypress.co.uk